THE

OF

SOUTHERN

CALIFORNIA

THE
GARDENS
OF

SOUTHERN

CALIFORNIA

PHOTOGRAPHS BY MELBA LEVICK

TEXT BY HELAINE KAPLAN PRENTICE

CHRONICLE BOOKS • SAN FRANCISCO

Printed in Japan.

Book design: Marquand Books, Inc.
Editing: Carey Charlesworth

Permission to reproduce the photographs on pages 217–221
courtesy of Rancho Santa Ana Botanic Garden.

Library of Congress Cataloging in Publication Data
Levick, Melba.
    The gardens of Southern California / photographs by Melba Levick :
  by Helaine Kaplan Prentice.
      p.   cm.
    Includes index.
    ISBN 0-87701-709-3
    1. Gardens — California, Southern. 2. Gardens — California,
Southern — Pictorial works. 3. California, Southern — Description and
travel. I. Prentice, Helaine Kaplan. II. Title.
SB466.U65C25   1990
712'.09794'9 — dc20   90-2311

Distributed in Canada by Raincoast Books, 112 East Third
Avenue, Vancouver, B.C., V5T 1C8

10 9 8 7 6 5 4 3 2 1

Chronicle Books
275 Fifth Street
San Francisco, California 94103

CONTENTS

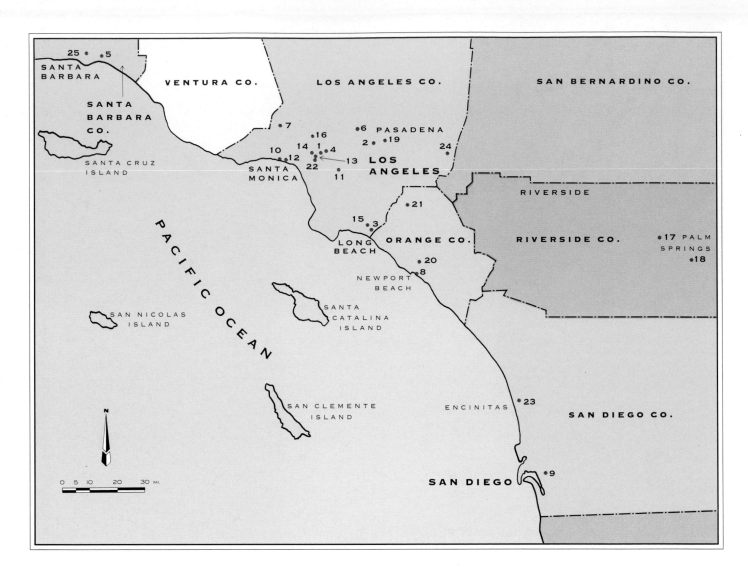

FEATURED GARDENS

ESTATES

1. Virginia Robinson Gardens
2. The Huntington Library, Art Collections, and Botanical Gardens
3. Rancho Los Alamitos
4. Greystone Park
5. Lotusland

HORTICULTURAL CENTERS

6. Descanso Gardens
7. Orcutt Ranch Horticulture Center
8. Sherman Library and Gardens
9. Balboa Park

SPECIAL PURPOSE GARDENS

10. The J. Paul Getty Museum
11. Exposition Park Rose Garden
12. Self-Realization Fellowship Lake Shrine
13. Franklin D. Murphy Sculpture Garden, UCLA

JAPANESE GARDENS

14. The UCLA Hannah Carter Japanese Garden
15. Earl Burns Miller Japanese Garden
16. Donald C. Tillman Water Reclamation Plant Japanese Garden

DESERT GARDENS

17. Moorten Botanical Garden
18. The Living Desert

BOTANIC GARDENS

19. Los Angeles State and County Arboretum
20. UC Irvine Arboretum
21. Fullerton Arboretum
22. The Mildred E. Mathias Botanical Garden, UCLA
23. Quail Botanical Gardens

CALIFORNIA NATIVE PLANT GARDENS

24. Rancho Santa Ana Botanic Garden
25. Santa Barbara Botanic Garden

INTRODUCTION

There was a time lasting well into this century when the central image of Southern California was its astonishing landscape. The soil and climate were so hospitable that, following discovery by Western explorers, the southland became an unfenced garden for magnificent exotic plants, including the palms, citrus, eucalyptus, and pepper trees that seem indigenous now. The romance of an earthly paradise where anything would grow led to the unstemmable expansion that has all but deluged the divine, original vision. Yet in the many public gardens of Southern California the truth behind the Edenlike mystique survives.

The public gardens convey a sense of place no building or monument ever could. They preserve and distill the fabled landscape that was celebrated unabashedly during the heydey of boosterism. "My California!" extolled one ode. "To be where honeybees hum melodies and orange trees scent the breeze."

The accolades were nothing new. By the late 1700s the *huertas*, or produce gardens of the Franciscan missions, had already become centers of agricultural productivity and, by extension, ornamental delight. Shipborne plant novelties from Pacific ports in South America and Asia flourished alongside native plants and Mediterranean introductions from Spain by way of Mexico. When Edwin Bryant visited Mission San Fernando in 1846, he recorded this impression, as cited by Victoria Padilla in *Southern California Gardens:*

> There are two extensive gardens, surrounded by high walls; and a stroll through them a most delightful contrast from the usually uncultivated landscape we have been travelling through for so long a time. Here were brought together most of the fruits and many of the plants of the temperate and tropical climates. Although not the season of flowers [January], still the roses were in bloom. Oranges, lemons, figs, and olives hung upon the trees, and the blood-red tuna, or prickly pear, looked very tempting.

Within the formidable borders that contain Southern California—mountains, two deserts, and the sea—the land soon came to resemble what Bryant had

seen within the mission walls, then just as rapidly succumbed to urbanization. In the Los Angeles Basin, surging freeways and an assertive street grid have usurped the arable coastal plain. Development has assaulted hillsides and arroyos, and intrusions stand out unforgiven in the open chapparal. Nonetheless, the portrayal of Southern California as a garden land endures. Every year, in the brilliant sunshine of New Years' Day, the flower-covered caravan of the Rose Bowl parade is broadcast live for all the shivering nation to see.

Garden history is human history. Dramatic characters, larger than life and at home in the freewheeling southland with its love for extravagance and drive, are the protagonists of many of the garden tales in this volume, from Cactus Slim to bigwigs like Huntington, Doheny, and Sherman, who were so closely allied with the development of Southern California that they are namesake to everything from beaches and boulevards to cities. The roster of determined women, from Susanna Bixby Bryant to Mildred E. Mathias, is equally impressive. They guided to fruition important botanic and estate gardens before women's leadership was accepted in other realms.

During the exuberant period from 1880 to the early 1930s, opportunists

came here by the carload, and an enterprising few became railroad barons, oilmen, and movie moguls. Such individuals could own hundreds of acres and proclaim their arrival in fabulous gardens. A phenomenal, broad-based interest in horticulture made plant collections a status symbol of the landed gentry and gardening an avid pastime of the common man. Introduction of nursery stock of every description was the passion of talented plant breeders, a vocation highly valued by the community. In gardens large and small, a fresh cast of flamboyant trees from mild latitudes was assembled alongside the native sycamores and live oaks.

Botanic gardens, although conceived for science and education, provided the seclusion, exotic verdure, and inspirational trees previously reserved for the privileged few on estates. As environmental awareness has grown, many botanic gardens have become preserves for threatened species, promoters of California native plants, and champions of global ecology.

Travelers expect to find great gardens where civilization and culture thrive. Los Angeles has emerged in our lifetime as a world city, and it is timely to recognize that garden destinations affirm the region's coming of age as much as do museums, theaters, and concerts halls. A galaxy of diverse and stellar gardens awaits your visit. In addition to estate and botanic gardens, there are Japanese gardens, sculpture gardens, desert gardens, historic re-creations, and specialty collections. A geographic directory at the

end of this book identifies some sixty smaller gardens in Southern California that complement the twenty-five featured entries. All are open to the public.

The public gardens need our support. They are dependent upon fund-raising, volunteer groups, and admission fees, and for these they must compete with an infinity of pastimes in Southern California to attract a following. Some gardens find themselves surrounded by residential neighborhoods that object to a public use in their midst and so seek restricted access. At the time of this writing, Lotusland, the extraordinary Montecito estate bequeathed for public enjoyment by Madame Ganna Walska, had not yet received a permit to open on a regular basis due to neighborhood opposition. Ironically, gardens like Lotusland established the air of exclusivity and luxury that opponents of public access so jealously guard.

Gardens rely more heavily on their caretakers than any other art form. When I visited the Fullerton Arboretum it was the day before a gathering of Southern California garden administrators. From beneath an open-sided canvas tent, neat rows of white folding chairs looked toward the citrus and avocado orchard. Although I would be on to yet another garden by the time the conference convened, I could visualize it. I had met and interviewed most of the next day's participants. They are exceptional individuals whose dedication and vision are the mainstay of their institutions. Aided by the availability of a large

immigrant labor pool that makes well-tended public gardens feasible, these administrators steward what remains of Southern California's landscape heritage.

It is an indisputable relief to arrive at the gates of these lush and luminous garden retreats, set apart from the city and several degrees cooler for the shade and moisture. It feels so good to be out of doors, walking and walking, propelled by one visual delight after another. Shortly you tune in to the natural world, but it is wonderfully civilized here as well, an ensemble of human endeavor and nature's gifts. Intensely stimulating flower hues, beguiling fragrance, a rightly framed view all claim your attention. Familiar plants take on new meaning; unknown and incredible species appear. Proud trees and spreading lawns, the restorative green, erase any lingering harsh sensations. As you stroll or rest, the sun-filled garden reveals the qualities of paradise that so many look for and never find in Southern California.

ESTATES

VIRGINIA ROBINSON GARDENS

BEVERLY HILLS

In the wealthy enclaves of great cities, imposing houses conceal gardens of privilege that are off limits to the ordinary tourist. The sting of exclusion from garden pleasures is keen on a daytime drive through Beverly Hills, where front yards are grandiose and gardeners omnipresent. But thanks to the largesse of Virginia Robinson, there is a breach in the barricade of mansions, and you are invited onto her estate to tour the grounds.

Through the porte-cochere and up the drive you go, past a thicket of palms so dense that you cannot discern where the jungle ends. You round the tennis court and rose garden and discover the guest house, a fine pavilion with an open-air Palladian motif. This is the pivotal garden structure. It anchors the outdoor play and entertainment spaces and surpasses in beauty and grace the 1911 Robinson residence. (The first estate home in Beverly Hills, it was designed by Mrs. Robinson's father and is now undergoing restoration.) The 1924 pavilion is serene and balanced, framed by strawberry trees and ornamented with buff-pink sgraffito nymphs between the Tuscan arches. Its Roman facade is backdrop to an idyllic swimming pool, sparkling turquoise blue.

In the loggialike cardroom overlooking the pool is a scrapbook with a newspaper announcement of the sudden wedding uniting Harry Robinson, son of the founder of Robinson's Department Store, and the "dainty, illusive Miss Virginia Dryden, Jr." "SIX DAYS WAS SHE ENGAGED," scolds the headline in mock rebuke. "Long list of admirers left in lurch by unexpected marriage." A coquettish photo follows of Virginia Robinson in white garden attire, standing alongside a freshly staked row of Italian

cypress, stiff as rods. She sports an ankle-length skirt, a sunhat whose brim is shoulder wide on her narrow frame, and a newlywed's grin of unrestrained delight.

Twenty matching specimen cypress now replace the trees in the photo, part of an active program to reinstate the garden as a showplace. Inevitable symptoms of age challenge the renovation: shade in unwanted places, plants of declining vigor, remnants of an archaic irrigation system, and some structural decay. But overall the garden is intact, and notably, it persists in residential form. Walkways and garden rooms have not been reconfigured to better accommodate groups; seasonal color has not been scattered willy-nilly for audience appeal; and there are no research foundations here or other extraneous occupants.

In fact, walking down from the cypress-flanked mall it feels so much as if our hostess were about to emerge in greeting that it is a disappointment to discover that Virginia Robinson died in 1977, six weeks shy of her one hundredth birthday. Her husband's survivor since 1934, she was supremely skilled in the diplomacy of wealth as practiced in Beverly Hills. For sixty-six years the house and garden were her social arena. She bequeathed them to the County of Los Angeles with an endowment of one million dollars for upkeep and the stipulation that the estate be used as a botanic garden.

The spine of the six-acre hilltop site is a formal alignment of house, lawn, pool,

and pavilion. From there, however, symmetry is dispensed with, and paths disperse to thematic terraces on the sides of the slope that are as different in character as they are in orientation. The plan was conceived by Charles Gibbs Adams, the Pasadena landscape architect well versed in European prototypes who catered to a well-heeled clientele.

The citrus garden, on a sunny south-facing slope, is a series of architectural landings stepping down the hill, replete with balustrades, statuary, and in a faint echo of the great Villa Lante in Bagnaia, a runnel for flowing water to fuel the fountains below. In summer, the scent of an unusual Central African gardenia *(Gardenia thunbergia)* envelops this spot. Look, too, for *Camellia japonica* 'Virginia Robinson' on a middle tier, named for her by Nuccio's Nursery in 1957. A shady, northerly slope, a contrast to this bright one, has an aviary and an informal woodland.

Guided tours here allow you to feel like Mrs. Robinson's personal guest. Their small size is the solution to neighborhood concern about the traffic that would accompany unlimited public access to the estate. Unfortunately, restrictive quotas imposed on attendance make it difficult to amass a garden constituency, and the hours of operation plainly exclude visitors who cannot attend on weekdays.

While the gardens are preserved, they will not be frozen in time. The Los Angeles State and County Arboretum, well known for its work with plant

introductions and charged with administering the grounds, will continue Mrs. Robinson's practice of testing new subtropicals, taking advantage of the benign microclimate on the hill. Virginia Robinson was an avid collector of rare and untried material. She wanted a wild, romantic garden and she planted densely, as her well-thumbed nursery catalogues and corresponding sales receipts attest.

Landscape architect Morgan Evans has used that documentation to design a master plan, which proposes an intriguing list of subtropical species that Mrs. Robinson had evidently pursued but for one reason or another have perished. It urges removal of intrusive plants and the return to prominence of the most exotic trees on the property, such as Jamaican earpod *(Enterolobium cyclocarpum)*, Guatamalan devil's hand *(Chiranthodendron pentadactylon)*, an Indian bamboo *(Bambusa beecheyana)* whose culms far exceed in size the varieties common in California, and a white-flowered Kauaian hibiscus *(Hibiscus arnottianus)*.

Nowhere is Mrs. Robinson's taste for aristocratic species more apparent than on the east-facing slope where she planted the stately king palm *(Archontophoenix cunninghamiana)* endemic to the east coast of Australia. Conditions so favored regeneration that a tropical forest grew. The pattern of overlapping fronds casts shadows on the glossy trunks like the barred light of venetian blinds. Within, it is cool, dim, and except for the orange

lanterns of kaffir lily lighting the path, entirely green. Even the bark of king palms is green, royal green. "The sun won't find me here," sighed a model who appeared during my tour, perspiring and seeking refuge from the intense heat of a fashion shoot on the tennis court.

This is more than the largest collection of king palms outside Australia—it is an environment with an ecology of its own: a layered canopy fifty to sixty feet overhead and, sprouting in the groundcover of ferns, volunteer king palms everywhere. There was a time that the screech of monkeys could be heard within. Now, it is ideal for the acclimatization of shade-tolerant palm species by the arboretum.

The palm jungle merges with other subtropical plants, including kentias, arecastrums, ginger, and two magnificent aerial-rooted Australian figs (*Ficus rubiginosa var. australis*). Confronting what was once a fabulous allée of king palms is the East Overlook, a secluded terrace furnished with turtle-footed wrought iron chairs where Virginia Robinson would retire to read. It is a place conducive to picturing the foresighted woman whose invitation has made your visit possible.

THE HUNTINGTON LIBRARY, ART COLLECTIONS, AND BOTANICAL GARDENS

SAN MARINO

When Henry E. Huntington did things, he did them big and he did them right. An incessant worker and skillful industrialist, he transformed inefficient factories, built railroads across hostile terrain, expanded interurban transit in San Francisco and Los Angeles, developed electric power, and in acquiring real estate became the greatest single landowner in his day in Southern California. He managed large-scale enterprise, deploying legions of workmen and bringing about dramatic, perceptible change. So it was that beginning in 1903, when he set out to improve his own ranch, a six-hundred-acre tract overlooking the San Gabriel Valley, his vision for the garden and the scope of alteration to the land took on the magnitude of a public works project. That was simply how Huntington operated.

Improvements for the first two years were directed toward the laying of an extensive drainage system. An on-site nursery, established to grow the tremendous quantities needed for mass plant-ings, soon produced more than fifteen thousand plants. To stabilize a four-acre slope for the Palm Collection, three-hundred thousand *Lippia repens* were planted. The large numbers of matching California pepper and Guadalupe Island palm trees used to define boundaries and to line drives were tantamount to municipal-street tree installations. An existing four-million-gallon reservoir was repeatedly augmented, until capacity was more than doubled. For the convenience of car-lot delivery of construction materials Huntington installed a private spur track. Thus when porous rock was needed to enhance a setting for semi-tropicals, two open steel freight cars

filled to capacity with tufa stone were summoned from Santa Cruz directly to the ranch.

Captains of industry like Henry E. Huntington had trusted lieutenants to carry out orders and stay up sleepless nights figuring out how to accomplish by tomorrow some insuperable task that had been casually requested today. On the San Marino Ranch, that man was William Hertrich. A German trained in the old-world craft of landscape gardening, Hertrich had taken a horticultural apprenticeship in Austria and studied estate management. He was a consummate plantsman, from propagation to tree moving, and an intuitive engineer, from earthwork to erosion control. An able administrator possessed of an inquiring intellect, he thrived in this position. What is remarkable is H. E. Huntington's good fortune in engaging the extraordinary Hertrich, for few, if any, others would have been equal to the job. In fact, it was Hertrich, sensing the rosy future of the Los Angeles area, who sought Huntington out, not the other way around.

"Hertrich," you can hear Huntington commanding genially, "see what you can do with these." He hands his man a pocketful of wooden eggs that he had procured from the chef at the Jonathon Club, the patrician reserve in Los Angeles where he was residing during early improvements to the ranch. Hertrich recognized avocado pits, and confident that he could propagate the fruit his employer so much enjoyed, immediately planted the seeds in pots. Thus began the first avocado orchard in Southern California, the nucleus of the avocado industry. This was, after all, a commercial orchard operation, complete with packinghouse. Trees remaining from the original experiment can be seen at the northern end of the parking lot.

"Hertrich," you can hear Huntington asking directly, "Is it possible to transplant large trees? I want this place to look finished as soon as possible." And so, Hertrich tells us, at considerable risk to himself but with marked success in the landscape, he "transplanted desirable trees from wherever they could be found; some of them stood thirty to fifty feet high and weighed from ten to twenty tons apiece." Trees were brought from other Huntington properties in the Pasadena area and from elsewhere in Los Angeles. *Cocos plumosa* was transported on flat cars from San Diego, and two charred palms that had stood near the San Francisco home of Collis P. Huntington (destroyed by the earthquake and fire of 1906) had wholly recovered by 1910 in

San Marino. The equipment was primitive, the ranch hands and horse teams inexperienced at this sort of work, and the maneuvering dangerous. It is no wonder that Huntington would watch tree-moving procedures "with evident interest and often deep concern."

"Hertrich," you can imagine Huntington stating forthrightly, "I like your idea. But it must be done by winter." Six months had been Hertrich's estimate for transforming a small canyon and reservoir into a Japanese garden. It was already summer 1912. Huntington wanted the work complete as a gift to his new wife, Arabella, before the family's anticipated move into the new residence. Hertrich's crew went to work at once, leveling the dam, erecting the rockery and waterfall, excavating for ponds, "with the bare possibility in mind that it would be sufficiently finished in time to be a source of satisfaction."

For mature Oriental plants he searched desperately in the nurseries, at last approaching the owner of a commercial Japanese tea garden in Pasadena, who politely declined to sell his full-grown trees and shrubs but willingly accepted an offer to purchase the entire operation—ornaments, fixtures, and all. Four crews, dividing the labor of digging, boxing, transporting, and transplanting the coveted plants, made fast work of the job. The garden was substantially complete in three months' time, although occupancy of the house—some things never change—was delayed until January 1914, an entire year.

The Japanese Garden has a picture-postcard quality, the vermilion drum bridge in its tranquil valley the most photographed scene in the Huntington Gardens. Seasoned photographers, framing the view with pendant wisteria blossoms from the bowered terrace above, would regret to learn that unpainted bridges are more traditional in Japanese gardens, for who could relinquish this classic Kodachrome image of red against green? Equally picturesque was the Japanese family employed in Huntington's time to maintain the garden and live in the two-story house erected at the far side of the garden, a variation on sixteenth-century Shoin-style architecture. On holidays, the parents and three children would dress in traditional costume and stroll the circuit of paths.

As Hertrich tells it in an illuminating book called *Personal Recollections* from which the quotations above are taken, the garden superintendent was asked to do most everything, sooner or later. The mushrooming roster of duties is hilarious, from conjuring up a method to haul a 148-foot-tall Oregon-fir flag pole from the harbor at Redondo Beach to canvassing for the requisite five hundred signatures to incorporate the city of San Marino. One winter he was obligated to break into Mrs. Huntington's locked closet to rescue her wardrobe from a leaky pipe, then repair the offending plumbing and, lest her peace of mind be disturbed, secretly replace the closet door hinges and touch up the paint. But

his frustration must have been real. The horticultural agenda of a man like Hertrich would have been a full-time endeavor and time only reluctantly diverted from it.

In the early twentieth century, men of position and means in Southern California indulged horticultural passion as today they might buy a professional sports franchise, and Henry E. Huntington was exemplary among them. The gardens surrounding the lavish residence (now art gallery) are acclaimed for botanical depth and ornamental brilliance, but they were never a wifely domain, notwithstanding the aviary built for Mrs. Huntington's amusement and her well-used cut-flower garden. Due to poor eyesight she required overscaled flower arrangements, presaging those now favored in fashionable restaurants. Fifty to two hundred blooms would be used in a single container, quantities of which were dispersed in the palatial house and on the loggia. Even today, the grounds do not have a domestic air but are like a glorious park, with composed views of statuary and stone temples in an English tradition that suits the British

theme of the art collection, the library holdings, and the neoclassical architecture.

Magnificent spreading oaks cast deep pools of shadow on a seemingly limitless lawn, its boundary hidden beyond the horizon of the hill. The venerable English oak (*Quercus robur*) and the cherished Pasadena oak (*Q. engelmannii*) are the trees of pedigree and substance here, comparable to the noble cedars of Lebanon that guard the stately homes of England. Living coats of arms, they are symbols of history and lineage in scale with the grandest hall but none too large for the demesne. Huntington treasured the oaks on the property, undertook

experimental surgery to save damaged ones, would be found at six in the morning walking among them, and chose to sit in their midst to discuss future plans and recount his past with Hertrich.

Huntington had first seen this property on a propitious visit in 1893 when relocating to San Francisco from the East Coast. At sunset, from the deep, bracketed recesses of the Victorian porch at the de Shorb residence, he surveyed the surroundings and was smitten by the views obtained from the rise. Once having acquired the well-disposed site, Huntington forsook other properties within his extensive real estate holdings, directing that the de Shorb house be

disassembled and the lumber used to construct six four-room laborers' dwellings on the ranch.

To the north of the manse, two rows of rarely seen fountain palms (*Livistona decipiens*) and a procession of allegorical statuary frame an axial view of the San Gabriel Mountains. This formal garden area, called the North Vista, is slightly out of alignment with the house (due to a belated decision to save certain oaks), as is the rose garden and its tempietto. An imposing, ceremonial veranda where the Victorian porch once stood commands the valley view to the south.

One Sunday afternoon, Huntington and Hertrich sat in the shade of a group of California sycamores. To Hertrich's request for permission to establish a cactus garden, Huntington evinced complete surprise and a little horror. He "thoroughly disliked all types of cacti," having had a painful encounter with one while supervising construction of the Southern Pacific Railroad in the Arizona Desert. Hertrich persisted, citing scientific and educational value, climatic opportunity, the uniqueness of the collection. Then, one pragmatic man to another, Hertrich pointed to an unsightly hillside in plain view of the main drive

with soil too barren for most plantings, and pronounced it the ideal location for a cactus garden. His case was made.

Once established, the Desert Garden gave Huntington great pleasure as a showplace. Later expanded to twelve acres with some twenty-five hundred different species, it has achieved international importance as an outdoor collection and for its planting design.

The Desert Garden comes into view like a reverse mirage, a vision of dryness in the verdure. Approach it from the lily ponds and the luxuriant greensward of cone-bearing trees, many rare, like the Kashmir cypress (*Cupressus cashmeriana*) with foliage draped like strands of tinsel. By this route the contrast between pliant and prickly, moist and arid is far more dramatic than when approaching the Desert Garden along the concrete walkway and past the rock wall from the entry arcade.

The Desert Garden is a hard-edged landscape of surfaces and forms. Otherworldly, it has been likened to the bottom of a waterless sea, the encrusted surface of a distant planet, a remake of *Fantasia*. But it is far more than an extensive collection of botanic oddities adapted to hot, dry conditions. What distinguishes this as a "garden" is that the plants are arranged for esthetic impact, and not by family or natural distribution. The cacti and succulents are massed in generous, almost ostentatious quantities of a single type, achieving what could be called ultratexture. A sampling of pincushion

cactus (*Mammillaria* spp.) is always intriguing. Its spiralling rows of tubercles occur in the natural proportion, known as the "golden mean," so pleasing to the eye that it has been imitated in architecture since the Parthenon. But when countless numbers of the protuberant creatures swarm over red lava rock, as here, they coalesce into an undulating landform.

In this Desert Garden, all plants, whether common or rare, are positioned for height and form the way trees, shrubs, and groundcover would be combined in more typically terrestrial settings. For example, the spiking inflorescence of the agave and the columnar saguaro are arboreal in form. The plumelike beaucarnea and the hefty golden barrel cactus are like ornamental shrubs of different size and mien. Filling out at ground level are that writhing serpent called creeping devil (*Stenocereus eruca*), the repetitive rosettes of crassulas, sedums, sempervivums, and the spineless living-rock cactus (*Ariocarpus fissuratus*). Fifty or so species of noncactus trees and shrubs,

like the yellow-flowered cassias, modulate the scene and provide needed shade for certain cactus species. One graceful, white-trunked sycamore, a Desert Garden landmark, I take to be of the grouping where Huntington and Hertrich conversed.

Then there are the unexpected combinations of color. Silvery white wool and russet haloes on golden spines. Glacial blue agave spears, the yellow banded aloe, the glossy, deep maroon of black aeonium grown in full sun and slightly underwatered, to bring out the menacing hue of this unusual sport. Notwithstanding the pink neon mats of flowering iceplant and the aquamarine of *Puya alpestris,* little of the color is floral.

In business, Huntington abided by high standards—a trait along with independence that endeared him to his uncle, railroad baron Collis P. Huntington, who gave Henry his start—and that approach imbues the cultural facility he created. The Huntington Library, Art Collections, and Botanical Gardens, as the whole is called, is run with an eye to perfection befitting royalty. It is one thing to successfully manage a 207-acre domain with a prodigious research library, renowned art collections, and 15 distinct gardens, any one of which would be an attraction in its own right, and in doing so to satisfy half a million visitors annually. It is altogether another to do it to the utmost. Not only acreage and holdings but also scrupulous standards and attention to detail set the Huntington apart.

The maintenance and expansion of scientifically valid plant collections is a prime objective here, with active research in certain genera, more than fourteen thousand different kinds of plants, and an impressive array of unusual species. The book *Exceptional Trees of Los Angeles* lists numerous outstanding species on the property, including the Atlantic blue cedar from which all others are descended (*Cedrus atlantica 'Glauca'*). Strawberry snowball (*Dombeya cacuminum*) and macadamia nut (*Macadamia integrifolia*) are two exotics among several at the Huntington described as the first, biggest, or only example in California. Technical improvements in record keeping are underway, notably computerized mapping of every plant in every bed and recording of sixty-five thousand accession cards. Time-honored methods thrive as well: a horticultural library with historic nursery catalogues, a slide collection, and an herbarium. When I looked in on the lab, one technician was jostling with computer graphics to display

the irrigation network while another was trying bemusedly to press a sample that looked like a bottlebrush made of toothpicks and reduce its insistent three dimensions to two.

Behind the desk of Botanical Gardens curator James Folsom, as we discussed design and management issues, I noticed two dictionaries, one German, the other Spanish; they are as essential to his work as *Hortus Third*. The superintendent, Fred Brandt, is East German and the garden crew primarily Hispanic. "Ola!" the curator calls automatically to every laborer we see as we range through the grounds, he the official escort but clearly doing double duty to inspect operations in the manner of Huntington or Hertrich. Folsom too is at one with the institution and its grounds. "We are in the counterculture," he observes wryly of an administration whose ideals hark back to an earlier era. "Dealing with the future facing four-squarely backward."

That gardens are a tug-of-war with nature is obvious, but the truth of the statement is magnified several times over at the Huntington by the size of the property and the intensity with which 150 acres are developed. When the Santa Ana winds strike with their northeasterly gusts every year, twenty to one hundred trees are lost. To combat vermin, there has always been a full-time gopher killer on staff. And to satisfy a thirsty plant collection, three hundred acre-feet of water are needed every year. With a masterful stroke, the Huntington

board recently purchased additional water rights from a defunct industrial user, the only way the botanic garden could increase its water entitlement.

We walked to the mausoleum—the ultimate garden structure, if you will. Among the citrus groves, behind the delicate tracery of wrought iron gates and atop a long, straight drive stands a monument that would look at home in Washington, D.C. A white marble rotunda designed by John Russell Pope, architect of the Jefferson Memorial and the National Gallery of Art, is adorned with simplicity by the lemon-scented eucalyptus (*E. citriodora*), its trunk as smooth and white as cool Carrara. Within the circle of Ionic columns, the four apocryphal stages of life are depicted as seasons. It is remote and meditative here, and I imagine that Jim has come to communicate, to learn what the benefactor would like to see improved. "Folsom," you can almost hear Huntington calling, "the lily ponds

should be relined." And, "Folsom, about the conservatory. Kew has just restored theirs, it is time to attend to ours. Where do you recommend it be constructed?"

The goal at the Huntington Botanical Gardens is to carry on as an estate. Protecting the openness of the landscape is essential—hedges, for example, are proscribed along paths. Incredibly, although it might seem otherwise to the footworn at closing time, the property is filling up. Features have been removed since Huntington's day—the turtle pond, the lath house, Arabella's aviary, and others—but major new gardens and collections have been introduced and original installations grown large in maturity. How different the garden seems compared to earlier times; old photos have the skeletal look of lithographs of Vaux-le-Vicomte when it first began.

Hertrich's tenure continued for twenty-one years after Huntington's death—forty-four years in all—and even after retirement in 1948 he continued to call the shots. Author of numerous books, including a three-volume work on camellias—hence the vast camellia collections adjoining the Japanese Garden and the North Vista—William Hertrich had become an expert on cycads, palms, orchids, and desert plants, and an important figure in Southern California horticultural circles.

Since his time, numerous changes and additions have occurred. The impression of the enclosed Zen Garden, added in 1965–66, is engraved in my memory from a visit long ago, like the lines raked into the gravel. In early morning or late afternoon, shadows define the etching that at midday practically disappears. This is the *karesansui,* or dry-style garden, and the viewer is invited to gain a more specific awareness of nature by association. Fortunately, there is a plaque decoding the garden symbols. Raked patterns represent water flowing from a cascade; the gray slate walk, a bank on the edge of a sea. The sculpted shrubbery mimics low rolling hills; a small stand of gingko trees, the forest; and so forth.

Other additions include the Australian collection, the Jungle Garden, the Subtropical Garden, the refurbished Rose Garden, and a "cactarium." The Shakespeare Garden complements library holdings, its wide, central swale of flowers like a perennial border turned outside-in. In an atypical lapse in judgment, the cut-flower garden so characteristic of the Huntingtons' occupancy was replaced by a brick-entombed herb garden. Every major garden has its own curator and permanently assigned gardeners: there is far more than can be covered in one visit or a profile of this sort.

As Huntington intended, the public is the true beneficiary. Limited operating hours may appear exclusionary (they are in part a response to attendance quotas imposed by the City of San Marino), but the outcome is that all maintenance can be conducted behind the scenes — clippings to dump stations by 11:30; last trash call at 12:30 — so that when the gates open at 1:00, a picture-perfect afternoon is bestowed upon the visitor. Less perfect is the method of supporting the botanical garden. Huntington failed to bequeath for it a specific endowment.

At the Huntington Botanical Gardens there is room for even the rich to dream. Not of hot tubs, tennis courts, or private pools, the mundane aspirations of modern, consumer culture, but the grand ambition of applying wealth to public service, of assuming responsibility and leadership to support science and culture, and in particular, to further the landscape arts.

RANCHO LOS ALAMITOS

There is a drum roll on the mesa, a tremendous sense of excitement and ambition in the garden. Rancho Los Alamitos, also known as the old Bixby Ranch, is on the eve of transformation from an undervalued resource to an energetically managed cultural asset of statewide importance. Seven-and-a-half cultivated acres are scant souvenir of the vast, semiarid spread of more than twenty-eight thousand acres held by John Bixby and his partners in 1881, but ranch house and office, barns and outbuildings, and, significantly, a sequence of hospitable outdoor rooms surrounding the residence remain. Furthermore, Rancho Los Alamitos is about to become the pillar of garden restoration in Southern California. On the strength of scrupulous research and analysis, it will serve as the definitive standard of accuracy for reconstructed historic landscapes. Finally, because the ranch and its environs exemplify so profoundly the past and present, the Rancho Los Alamitos Foundation will take on an interpretive program with a far-reaching theme: the march of time in this sprawling, transmuted region. They will call it "Island in a Sea of Change."

A gated residential neighborhood confining it like a moat, Rancho Los Alamitos is located on a rise above the broad plain of Los Angeles Basin. Like most gardens, it confers retreat from the hurly-burly metropolis below, but all the more, the old Bixby ranch is a surviving portrayal of California's composite cultural heritage. Long ago, according to historian David Lavender, a spring flowed from a lower slope of the hill, supporting such plant life as the small

cottonwoods—the *alamitos*—and drawing Gabrielino Indians to a gathering
place called Puvunga. Middens attest to a
community fed plentifully on shellfish,
and legend has it that the central figure of
their creation myth, Chinigchinich, was
born here at Puvunga.

During the Spanish period, the property was part of the largest land grant
ever bestowed by the Spanish or Mexican
governments—167,000 acres in 1790 to
Manuel Nieto. When the colorful
rancher Abel Stearns acquired the land
in 1842, it contained a crude adobe
dwelling, to which he added a bunkhouse
wing for his vaqueros. In an analogy to
the layers of history on the site, thick
adobe bricks still form the inner core of
the house that John and Susan Bixby
commenced to improve in the 1880s. On
a mesa that has been continually inhabited for fifteen hundred years there is a
powerful sense of place that transcends
any single period.

Fred Bixby inherited the working
ranch in 1906 and with wife Florence
raised a family of five in an atmosphere
tumbling over with life, animals, and
children. The Bixby family led an unpre-
tentious life, and the current project aims
to recapture the robustness and fun of
ranching. Rancho Los Alamitos was
known for annual June children's parties
at which nearly two hundred frolicsome
guests would experience a private country fair, replete with cart rides to the
beach drawn by family-bred shires. The
three Bixby daughters became cowgirl

debutantes, up at dawn to ride, rope, and holler, off to tennis in the afternoon—a court was constructed to enhance their social life—then on to a dance or society reception at night.

The ranch was not a sport of the wealthy but a family enterprise. Scaled back to thirty-six hundred acres in 1912 and redirected to cattle and associated fodder crops, it at last enjoyed prosperity when oil strikes at Signal Beach in 1921 and Seal Beach in 1926 fueled the family fortune. "Nothing fattens up a steer like rubbing up against the legs of an oil derrick" was Fred Bixby's elixir for success. The appearance of the restored gardens and ranch house will refer to these times, the 1920s and 1930s.

What distinguishes Rancho Los Alamitos is that unlike many other estates of the period, where the gardens were erected for status or show, the garden rooms here decidedly reflect the preferences of the owners. Restraint was always a family trait and, regardless of the change in means that accompanied the oil strikes, this held forth in garden design. There were sapote, grapes, and artichokes because the Bixbys liked to eat them, and because Florence liked blue flowers, *Solanum, Iochroma,* and blue plumbago. There is a Friendly Garden for cuttings Florence received from fellow enthusiasts, a Native Garden due to her prescient interest in native plants, and a Desert Garden, the unexpected outcome of an experiment with spineless cactus showing promise as cattle feed. Florence

became enamored of cacti and succulents, yet her collection has a residential rather than botanic-garden quality. A recent discovery in the Native Garden is an extensive rockery and water garden, which is being unearthed with archaeological dedication.

From the dusty days of her first arrival when a water wagon came around twice daily to keep the dirt down, Florence took up defining the boundary between ranch and home where Susan Bixby had left off. Susan was the first to civilize the area around the house, and she planted numerous shade trees. These remained as a framework for future garden spaces: pepper trees, emblem of

California ranch life, for the drive, and, to formalize the front of the house, a pair of clipped Monterey cypress with two small Moreton Bay figs between them.

Today the fig trees are immense. From massive but short buttressed trunks erupt a canopy of outstretched arms. One of Florence's first steps was to install a lawn in the province of the now lordly figs, and like other spaces immediatley around the house, it assumed a role for entertaining or daily use. The lawn became an outdoor party room, ringed with animal displays at the June celebrations and arrayed with red and white checkered tablecloths for ranch barbecues. (Fred made the barbecue sauce; meat awaiting the grill swung from the fig trees.) In the music room, Florence installed French doors to invite dancing on the adjoining patio. The music room once held a small Monet, now at the Los Angeles County Museum of Art, that complemented the water lilies in the fountain outside.

"We have pulled out every plant sign and there will not be another," Executive Director Pamela Seager assured me as we took the morning sun in Florence's Secret Garden. This is a seductive little gated courtyard, its white walls inset with ceramic plaques and brilliant with bougainvillea, the whole overhung by a timeworn pepper tree. "Visitors will experience the garden directly. It will feel like a home, not an institution." With warm flagstone beneath my feet, and chatting amiably, I settled back in the

green iron chair. It certainly felt like a home to me.

While Florence had the assistance of ranch hands and gardeners and, over time, hired a virtual roll call of Southern California's garden experts—William Hertrich, Allen Chickering, Ed and Paul J. Howard, Yoch and Council, Charles Gibbs Adams—the gardens are characterized by the constancy of Florence's spade-in-hand participation. A winsome detail of landscape architect Russell Beatty's restoration plan is placement of a worn, coiled red hose of the type Florence would have used in the rear-door garden, the everyday entrance to the house.

At about the time Fred's sister, Susanna Bixby Bryant, was developing a botanic garden at Rancho Santa Ana, a satellite of Rancho Los Alamitos, Florence was expanding her gardens to the south side of the entry drive. Desirous of new terraces there, Florence Bixby engaged Florence Yoch, the formidable landscape architect who would draw inspiration from European models but take an unexpected turn or bold departure. Yoch's use of opulent references is restrained in deference to the informality of Bixby Ranch, but the organization of the spaces and their human scale are typical of her most-admired work.

Yoch designed two parallel promenades, Geranium Walk and Oleander Walk, the first four feet or so below the driveway, the second, on a lower level, a straight brick walk flanked by tree-form oleander. Now full grown and leaning for

light, the oleanders have a motile, Van Gogh–like beauty. The low, rough-stucco walls at both levels (and repeated elsewhere on the grounds) are surmounted by clay pots and lend a Spanish air. The walks are joined together at one end by vertical, dark green cypress climbing a stairway and at the other end by a rustic gazebo, once roofed with palm fronds, overlooking a rose garden. At the time there was a view to the ocean from the gazebo; the endemic sense of plateau it gave is now best attained from the Jacaranda Walk, behind the tennis court. After deciding to retain the aged oleanders, the planned restoration of Oleander Walk became relatively simple: replace two mismatched oleanders with the double-pink variety to complete the allée, whitewash the walls, and fabricate a

missing terra-cotta urn to match its counterparts. A complete set of 1927–28 garden photographs guides the restitution of errant pots, urns, and statuary to original locations.

With a vigor for improvements to the ranch that was a Bixby tradition, Rancho Los Alamitos staff and consultants are digging in. Extensive archival research, oral histories, and even the screening of old home movies drive design decisions. Adhering to a policy framework based on the Secretary of the Interior's Guidelines for Historic Preservation earned Rancho Los Alamitos the first grant for landscape restoration from California's Office of Historic Preservation, and it is sizeable. Augmenting the house and garden restoration, the comprehensive plan includes curatorial management and retrieval of artifacts, including books, paintings, and furniture; restoration of the ranch office that occupies one wing of the house; and creation of an interpretive center alongside the repositioned barn and stable.

Rancho Los Alamitos is open to visitors, as it has been since 1970, with the garden spaces evocative and generally intact, if not refurbished. With any luck—also a Bixby tradition—additional funds will be procured by 1993 and the garden will be closed for eight months to complete the restoration.

GREYSTONE PARK

"Give them everything."

That was the directive landscape architect Paul Thiene gave his staff for the design of the Greystone estate. And that's what the Doheny family got. An English front lawn, an Italian back terrace, a rose garden, a swimming pool and pavilion, tennis and badminton courts, numerous fountains and garden art, two lakes, two waterfalls (one of them eighty feet high), a complete system of landscape illumination, and to sustain the conspicuous turf, the world's largest sprinkler system. The pithy quotation, epigraph to the *Greystone Historical Report* by chroniclers of Los Angeles history Charles Lockwood and Peter V. Persic, sums up a pleasure garden that was created on demand for an oil-rich client, then perpetually manicured by a small and industrious army. Although the estate's benefactor, E. L. Doheny, Sr., was a noted plant collector, there is nothing in the historic account to suggest that any family member had a personal landscape vision for Greystone.

The primary use of the Doheny gardens was to register social standing. That they were used for entertaining or recreation is a logical corollary.

It is hard to imagine that any less of a landscape could live up to the Doheny mansion. It had: fifty-five rooms; a Gothic church of a living room with a massive fireplace; a marble-floored card room with flowing fountain; iron grillwork forming the initials E.L.D.; archways of intricately carved and highly polished oak; a palatial stairway; a six-room master suite; a host of children's bedrooms, with a playroom and small kitchen nearby; a two-story servants' wing, with butler's pantry, kitchen, flower room, servants' dining room, maids' sitting room and maids' rooms on the first floor, then on the second floor a sewing room, linen room, more maids' rooms, and a gift room solely for wrapping Christmas presents; catwalks in the attic and passageways between walls for repair to plumbing and electrical systems; a rec center in the "basement" entered through the stone turret in one corner of

the arrival court, with movie projection room, billiard room, regulation bowling alley, and, hidden behind panelling that retracted into the ceiling at the push of a button (this being Prohibition), a bar; for a grand total of 46,054 square feet in the main house. Among the outbuildings were a firehouse with three fire engines; a seven-room stone gatehouse; a garage with gas pumps, lifts, and machine shop to make any necessary part for the dozen or so cars stored there, including a '34 Olds (one of two made), a '36 Lincoln Zephyr, two sixteen-cylinder '36 Cadillacs (of only twenty made); a thatch-roofed, four-room playhouse with everything including a grand piano reduced to child's scale; a kennel; a greenhouse; and a stable.

Edward Laurence Doheny amassed his considerable fortune as a prospector, though an unlucky one at first. He came to Los Angeles in 1892 at age thirty-six from Southwestern gold and silver fields to restock supplies, and with an uncanny instinct for any sign of money in the ground, he spotted from the window of a Victorian rooming house a wagon load of greasy brown chunks. Maybe it was the glint of sun on the oily "brea," or pitch, that caught his eye. In any event, Doheny caught up with the driver, asked about the load, and not long thereafter was on an empty neighborhood lot north of the downtown, digging a mining shaft.

With picks and shovels, Doheny and his mining partner sent a 5-by-7-foot

shaft down 155 feet, or deeper than a ten-story office building. "My grandfather was a tough old bird, I tell you, a tough old son of a gun," Timothy Doheny told Lockwood and Persic. Lacking a drill, those Bunyonesque characters chopped down a 60-foot eucalyptus tree and, sharpening one end of the trunk, went at it. At 460 feet they struck oil.

Thus began the epoch of the Los Angeles oil boom, and for Doheny—who sounds like an ornery Ruggles of Redgap in Timothy Doheny's reminiscence—a series of lucrative conquests in Fullerton, the Kern River Valley, and the wilds of Tampico, Mexico. Doheny also began to acquire Beverly Hills real estate and by 1914 had united ten parcels in a 429-acre ranch. (Five of the parcels were secured on his behalf by a brother-in-law, as the mention of the Doheny name drove prices up and fed suspicion about underground oil reserves.) A chapparal-covered hillside with a panoramic view, the Greystone site was parceled off from the ranch in 1925, a gift from Doheny to his only child, E. L. Doheny Jr., and construction for what would become the enclave of an extended family began.

The title Greystone is perilously close to Tarzan's Greystoke, and connotes a cardboard rendition of an English manor Hollywood style, but the place is solid as the proverbial rock. The walls of the house are three feet thick, of reinforced concrete on a steel frame, with a veneer of buff gray Indiana limestone. Noble stone dwellings of the landed gentry are generally Palladian in origin with columned porticoes, or they employ a medieval, Gothic imagery evolved from keeps and fortified castles, as here. When the younger Doheny's wife Lucy selected architect Gordon B. Kaufmann to design an English manor house, she exemplified the national taste in the late teens and twenties for period revival architecture. So happy was the family with the outcome that the architect was presented with a black and silver Cord as a token of their appreciation. (Unable to afford the maintenance, Kaufmann soon sold the rarefied automobile.)

The stone masonry of the terraces was the highlight of our visit. Stonework is an essential feature in many gardens—indeed there are European courtyards where stone is almost the solitary element—and Greystone is a good place to appreciate the craft. The Italianate terraces that reconfigure the slope behind the mansion are supported by handsome retaining walls faced with Indiana limestone, and offer a high-calibre example of ashlar masonry. Dressed, or squared off, blocks of stone distinguish ashlar from rubblework—the more common and informal craft in which irregular rock is laid in uncoursed walls. At Greystone, the mortar beds are tight and the walls are quarry-faced ashlar, an appealing rough texture enhanced by the random projection of occasional blocks. The stonework expresses its function visually: larger stones in the lower courses, narrower

ones toward the top, and limestone buttresses supporting the height of these critical walls.

The formal Italianate terraces are an intepretation of Renaissance prototypes. A pair of complex, curving stairways leads from a once-solid slate terrace — the central flower bed and lamppost are recent intrusions — to a rectangular, level lawn surrounded by stone balustrades and somber, upright yews. The shallow, stepped planes of blue Vermont slate at the threshold to the lawn are to be savored. A freestanding, tiered fountain serves as focal point, and the entire composition is set off against a backdrop of mature eucalypts. Parallel to and below this level is an allée called Cypress Walk, although the cypresses were long ago replaced by eugenia, and now these too are showing signs of distress. What is noteworthy about the gardens at Greystone is the extraordinary quality of materials. No expense was spared.

As if scripted by Agatha Christie, E. L. Doheny, Jr., was destined not to enjoy his father's gift. In 1929, within a year of taking occupancy, he was murdered by his personal secretary at Greystone. His wife and five children, joined three years later by her second husband, also an oil man, continued to live at Greystone until 1955, always grooming the landscape to the utmost. The property was then sold to Chicago executive Henry Crown, who leased it out as a movie location — over forty have been filmed here — but never lived on-site. The children grown, Lucy

Doheny Battson and husband Leigh Battson wanted something smaller for retirement and so constructed a twenty-seven-thousand-square-foot place nearby on ten acres called The Knoll.

In 1965, the City of Beverly Hills purchased the declining estate for use as a park and reservoir. It was the only available open space in town. Though the mansion was occupied for twelve years by the American Film Institute, it is mournfully vacant at present for want of neighborhood endorsement of a public or quasi-public use. Its empty halls, along with a shortage of interpretive material, account in part for a disturbing lack of focus on the premises.

Greystone no longer has "everything." The grounds have changed, and many features no longer exist. The blue-tiled swimming pool has been filled in with concrete, a sorry sight. Where the parking lot sits, on the reservoir roof, there had been a picnic meadow. The lakes and spectacular waterfall, the Cotswold playhouse, and various outbuildings that connoted an exclusive self-sufficiency are gone. But most apparent is the demise of meticulous upkeep. While it might not be possible for a public agency, even in image-conscious Beverly Hills, to attain the standards of a private garden, that change alone has escorted the surviving province of baronial Greystone across the boundary from privileged reserve to park.

LOTUSLAND

In European high society, a beguiling young woman devotes herself to the arduous study of operatic singing. Her beauty is captured on canvas and in sculpture. She attracts proposals of marriage from dukes, diplomats, and millionaires, eventually accepting no less than six offers. Far less favorable, however, are critical reviews of the soprano on stage. Although she garners leading roles, she struggles for artistic acclaim throughout her career, exhausting legions of voice teachers and pursuing by any means, however mystical or misguided, the tones that would stir an audience to ecstasy.

In her fifties, she redirects her romance and idealism to garden making on a newly acquired Southern California estate. This endevaor lasts until her hundredth year, and the gardens emerge, like the opera singer herself, opulent and emotive.

Lotusland is the thirty-seven-acre estate of Madame Ganna Walska. (This *nom de guerre* is prounounced with a "V" in her native Polish, but she is commonly referred to as "the Madame.") Behind a pink wall, a landmark on Sycamore Canyon Road in Montecito, is her garden of many parts. It is not classical, nor does it adhere, for the most part, to fashionable landscape treatments. To arrive at Lotusland after visiting Casa del Herrero down the road, a masterful Moorish garden but nonetheless orthodox in its allées and focal points, is to recognize the constraints of convention. To see the photographs in Winifred Starr Dobyns' *California Gardens* of the property called Cuesta Linda, which the Madame would purchase in 1941, is to marvel that

traditional garden imagery has been erased on much of the grounds. Observes editor W. George Waters in *Pacific Horticulture* of Lotusland, "How alike all other gardens now seem; how endlessly are old formulas repeated."

Through the wrought iron gate, the curving drive is lined with long-necked rosettes of green agave *(Agave attenuata)*, a succulent often seen in groups because the plant offsets readily from the stem, but used nowhere else as magnanimously as here. Plants in multiples, and an emphasis on texture and foliage, set the scene for what lies ahead.

The pink stucco villa gives on to a paved entry court in the Mediterranean manner. Odd treetops appear above the courtyard wall, the swordlike foliage of dragon trees. To either side of the handsome cast-stone portal, standing in for Italian cypress, are symmetrical shafts of cactus *(Neobuxbaumia polylopha)*. Golden ball and barrel cactus advance on the villa in droves. But all is upstaged by *Euphorbia ingens*, a spiny, flailing creature as tall as the house. Eccentric, perhaps, but this is a refined and aristocratic breed of nonconformity.

The cactus garden was designed by Ralph Stevens, a prominent Santa Barbara landscape designer who, so it happens, was born on this property. His father, pioneer nurseryman Kinton Stevens, had established home and business on the site in 1885, and assembled the first catalogue in California devoted to tropical and subtropical plants. Among

other unusual palms in the Lotusland collection of fifty-two species, the hefty Chilean wine palms *(Jubaea chilensis)* are the elder Stevens' legacy. Ralph Stevens was Ganna Walska's advisor until his death in 1958, but the results of their collaboration contain no small measure of what the Madame called, in another context, "the indispensable *elan* of my usually overgenerous nature."

Turn away from the house, and enter the lost world of the water lily ponds. Palms rise up behind banks of papyrus, taro, and jointed reeds. The cabana looks like a jungle had been cleared away to reveal a startling artifact of civilized settlement. When Lotusland was Cuesta Linda, the structure overlooked the swimming pool and vistas were framed by rows of juniper. Only potted citrus survived the transformation.

In the pond grow lotus, their leaves like parasols, and giant Amazon water lilies *(Victoria amazonica)*. Chartreuse platters with fluted, upturned edges of maroon look ample enough to float upon in meditation. Kinton Stevens introduced the lotus to California in 1893. The pink flower gives way to a woody fruit, and as it nods over, the seeds are dispensed like salt from a shaker to germinate easily in the mud below. A photograph of the villa in Ganna Walska's memoir, *Always Room at the Top*, is captioned Tibetland, but in another poetic renaming, she dubbed the estate Lotusland.

The Aloe Garden stages the unimagined possibilities of a familiar Southern

California ornamental. More than one hundred kinds of aloe enclose the space like a fantastic forest; combined in quantity are low-growing and arborescent forms, of which *Aloe bainesii* is the tallest. Flowers erupt in conical flames of orange and yellow. The foliage is hard edged, the impression strongly primitive. Surrounded by burnt-red tufa stone and black volcanic rock, the Aloe Garden suggests a time when plants were just beginning, before the eons created soil.

Prehistoric impressions recur elsewhere in the gardens in the swollen, scaly bases of *Beaucarnea recurvata* and in the collection of six hundred cycads, cone-bearing species that predate the appearance of flowering plants on earth. Through the grassy hillocks of the Cycad Garden a dinosaur might lumber to drink from the wallow.

The focus of the Aloe Garden is a shallow concrete pool edged with iridescent shells, like one of the many glittery costumes Ganna Walska wore on stage. The pale blue, ghostly pallor of the pool, set off against the dark cinders and shadowy succulents, appears as if illuminated by moonlight.

Abalone shells were plentiful in postwar Santa Barbara; at the local fishery they were heaped in mounds. Was Madame Walska the type who would have marched into the scrap yard there and commandeered the bounty? Hardly. She would have dispatched a courier with an irrefutable, "I must have those shells." The assignment fell to Oswald Da Ros, a

stonemason, and his first step upon securing them was to rid the pearlescent saucers of stench.

"The Madame hated yes-men," Da Ros informed me at his home on a balmy Santa Barbara evening. As the son of a mason, Da Ros first came onto the estate in 1942 and soon thereafter dared disagree with an edict from Ganna Walska. For this he earned her respect and a lifelong working relationship, but not until she was one up. Walska summoned the young Da Ros to the terrace adjoining the only wing of the house that she inhabited, called the pavilion — "I want to see you" — then ordered him to take a seat on a recently hosed white chair. Down he went into a puddle of water, but never gave her the satisfaction of his discomfort, or so she thought.

The shells are one expression of Madame's fondness for minerals and color, which are used to singular effect throughout the grounds. Another is the jewels she wore to an opening of the New York Metropolitan Opera in the 1940s: a diamond and emerald tiara, a diamond necklace, and two chains with emeralds the size of birds' eggs. At Lotusland, irregular chunks of blue-green glass trim paths like gargantuan gemstones. (It is slag from bottle manufacture.) The pebble mosaic near the Neptune Fountain is made of multicolored marble, not river rock. (To achieve the desired shape and smoothness, the pieces were tumbled in a cement mixer with granite sand.) Da Ros was unable to acquire the obsidian

Madame desired, but it was he who introduced uncut amethyst crystals to ornament the euphorbia garden.

Another signature element at Lotusland is the fearless use of blue plants. The Blue Garden, in particular — with its blue palm, blue cedar, blue spruce, and blue fescue lawn — exemplifies a performer's sensibility to mood.

In Paris, Madame Walska owned the Théâtre de Champs Elysées and produced musical works there. (To support this costly enterprise she named a perfume for herself; when the *parfumerie* where it was sold opened in 1927, traffic literally stopped on the Rue de la Paix to behold the couture and mogul's emerald she wore.)

At Lotusland there had to be a theater. It is an open-air performance space of semicircular grass tiers. These had been enclosed by a sheared cypress hedge, but, a victim of disease, it has been replaced by African boxwood. The proscenium arch and wings of the stage were replanted with podocarpus. As if a farce by Molière were underway, a troupe of seventeenth-century dwarf players, caricatures in stone imported from Madame's château Galluis, near Versailles, enlivens the Theater Garden.

Following a long sequence of dense and involved vegetation, including the Japanese Garden and other collections not mentioned here, the landscape opens up suddenly into a large bright lawn. It is a sight so welcome it has a buoying effect. Then it struck me: Madame Walska

must have waltzed through the gardens and up this greensward toward the villa singing her arias, singing to the sky, just as the sylphlike Duncan girls had danced in *galas champêtre* at château Galluis.

The heirloom on the green is a majestic Monterey cypress seen against the Santa Ynez Mountains. On one side the lawn is bordered by the surprise of large bromeliads and succulents. From an enormous live oak are suspended dozens of containers of donkey's tail *(Sedum morganianum)*. On the other side are flowers, formal gardens, topiary, and a floral clock. Additional touches no longer in evidence are the hammered bronze astrological signs that once marked the hours on the clock and a collection of carousel animals.

In 1958, Madame Walska prepared for Lotusland to become a center of horticultural significance after her death, unlike other important gardens that decline under subsequent owners, or are plundered. In 1984, the foundation she established assumed operation, endowed with a staff of curators and gardeners. At present, Lotusland is open on a very restricted basis and by group reservation only.

The Madame's *noblesse oblige* extended to the larger Santa Barbara landscape. When she noticed damaged palms on the shoreline at Cabrillo Boulevard, she funded their proper care, and she often opened her gardens to benefit Santa Barbara Beautiful.

On one such occasion in July of 1978, the Madame, who would be ninety-five next birthday, had promised that she would lead the first tour of the gardens. And so she did, a tiny figure with remarkably smooth skin beneath a big pink sunbonnet (she was also known for hats). Pinned to her blouse was an award of distinction bestowed by the French government. "Well into the tour," according to society columnist Beverly Jackson in the *Santa Barbara News Press*, "Madame Walska asked the entourage, 'Don't you love nature?' Everyone started to call out how beautiful the gardens were and how much they appreciated the privilege of viewing them. And to this she answered, with a smile slowly forming on the lips that had charmed heads of states and monarchs, 'Then why do you only photograph me?'"

HORTICULTURAL

CENTERS

DESCANSO GARDENS

LA CANADA FLINTRIDGE

The Descanso experience begins before the gate. Long, arching boughs of coast live oak line the curve of Descanso Drive, a serene and enviable residential street, forming a gracious entrance canopy to the gardens and, like a musical overture, intimating pleasures soon to come. For the heart of Descanso Gardens is the oak and camellia woodland, a perfect pairing of patriarchal native trees and introduced flowering understory, a horticultural match made in heaven.

The branches of the coast live oak and the arrangement of leaves temper the wind and rain and portion out the light. Fallen oak leaves are not removed, being a natural mulch that keeps the soil pH at a desirable level (between 5 and 6.5) for the acid-appreciative camellias. The hillside allows excellent drainage and the sandy loam provides soil aeration; all in all, a fair approximation of the camellias' natural habitat in the mountainous valleys of eastern Asia, where they coexist with rhododendron and azalea.

This is one of the largest camellia collections in the world. It is not a bedding out, as with roses, or a grouping of this and that species, as for botanic study, but a woodland chockablock with more than six hundred varieties of japonica, sasanqua, and reticulata species. You wend your way on cushiony, oak duff paths. Reduced to a child's level, your vision is blocked as in a topiary maze by the height of these shrubs, much larger than the suburban norm. Sprightly elves would surely fancy the waterfall and polka-dot profusion of winter bloom.

The camellias began as landscaping along the private drive to a twenty-two-room house built in 1938 by E. Manchester Boddy, owner and editor of the Los Angeles *Daily News*. He named his 165-acre ranch in a natural bowl of the San

Rafael hills for repose, Rancho del Descanso. This was a period of sky-rocketing recognition for camellias in Southern California, so Boddy, observing the ideal conditions for their culture on his oak-studded hillside, engaged J. Howard Asper, a camellia specialist from Los Angeles. Later, when his interests widened, Boddy brought on Dr. Walter E. Lammerts, an important hybridizer in state horticultural history, and with that, Descanso, contrary to its name, entered a period of indefatigable research and experimentation.

Lammerts developed and popularized the *Camellia reticulata,* a plant previously unknown here, with loose growth habit and remarkable peonylike flowers. In 1948 he imported the first collection from the Yunnan Province of China and subsequently, developed at Descanso eighteen distinct and elegant varieties. Boddy also ran a floral enterprise here, supplying Eastern markets with camellia foliage and blooms. Add to that the Ayreshire cattle he bred, and this was more than an estate for beauty's sake alone; it had purpose, scientific and commercial.

In Boddy's employ, Lammerts con-tinued work on deciduous fruit trees, ultimately breeding four superior peach trees for the home garden called 'Daily News.' For scent-starved East Coast emigrés he developed the lilac "Lavender Lady"; hence the lilac garden at Descanso today. But Lammerts' greatest contribution was in the realm of roses.

According to Victoria Padilla, Southern California's preeminent garden historian, it was Lammerts who took a difficult plant to grow and made it "one of the sturdiest denizens of the garden." The Descanso Rose History Garden is a living timeline of roses since Cleopatra, who ordered that the floors of her banquet halls be strewn with petals of *Rosa centifolia*.

Improvements to the rose garden are underway, the first step in implementation of a master plan prepared by the landscape architectural firm EDAW. Since its rescue from developers in 1957, Descanso has grown beyond camellias and roses with many features and programs added. The Van deKamp Educational Center (1982), built in the regional tradition of Craftsman architecture, and the Japanese Garden and Teahouse (1966) are examples of how support by the Descanso Gardens Guild has enriched a facility owned and operated by Los Angeles County, and introduced an atmosphere of refinement and decorum. Wisely, the master plan—also guild

funded—does not try to reshape the gardens, but concentrates on uniting the parts and improving some of the less successful of the numerous attractions. The birdwatching ponds, for example, are to be merged into a single water feature of size, and the tram is to be rerouted.

Twilight arrives. I can't believe my good fortune. The gates are closed, the public long since ushered back to reality at the closing hour, and here I am sharing the waning day with the man whose spirit far more than Boddy's or Lammerts' imbues Descanso now. George Lewis, superintendent of these gardens for nearly twenty years, is patiently watering an extravagant display of tulips—thirty-four thousand by his estimate—for the spring garden show. Some would tell you that tulips do not do well in warm climates, but George Lewis knows their secret. A native of New York and alumnus of Hampton College in Virginia, he is sixty-eight years old and widely acclaimed for his ability as plantsman and articulate teacher.

We are standing on a greensward, talking of things small and large. The late western light casts long shadows of California sycamore trunks diagonally across the lawn and spotlights two borders of undulating color: clear yellow, toasted orange, carmine, crimson, and more. As the light fades, the tulip petals fold together. They are like a phalanx of nuns, Lewis says of them, at eventide, in their shawls and praying to the heavens.

ORCUTT RANCH HORTICULTURE CENTER

Oaks and oranges. Of all the gardens, Orcutt caught us most by surprise. We weren't expecting an encounter with a vanished moment in California history. We had hopped a commuter airline, navigated three freeways, and followed an endless commercial strip where signs were bigger than buildings, and here we were, back in a time of ranches and orchards and uninterrupted space, thoroughly astonished. The day was very hot, the tropical scent of orange blossoms hanging low in the air.

Do not think that the Orcutt Ranch is a restoration. In fact, there are misguided improvements that would make a preservationist cringe. But what Orcutt gives up in precision it gains by total lack of affectation. What makes this ranch so real? The informal, even incidental grouping of outbuildings as you pull in the back gate off Roscoe Boulevard. The leaning, white-trunked sycamores, and the water fountain contrived from a length of terra-cotta sewer pipe. The denim-clad City of Los Angeles

employees who attend to practical matters of irrigation and maintenance at this and other parks in the West Valley District. They look on this stage for all the world like ranch hands. There are tractors and pickups, and derelict hot-air windmills once used to prevent low-lying frost from settling on the citrus groves. One was adjustable for the direction of the wind; the other was driven by a 1950 Ford flathead-six car engine, until someone paralyzed it with airplane fuel.

But let's start with the oaks, for that is where William and Mary Orcutt started in 1917 when they came from Los Angeles to vacation in a small cabin

under the towering trees. Orcutt was a geologist for the Union Oil Company, which must explain his choice of property. The layered red sandstone of the Santa Susanna mountains is vivid in the middle distance. The majestic valley oaks (*Quercus lobata*) and stately coast live oaks (*Q. agrifolia*), ancient on their native soil, invest the grassy landscape with a parklike character. When the Orcutts purchased the two-hundred-acre estate they named it *Rancho Sombra del Roble*, ranch in the shadow of the oak.

The oaks are yet the prophets of this place. A valley oak thirty-three feet in circumference near Dayton Creek is estimated at seven hundred years old; another near the rose garden measured eighteen feet in circumference back in 1974; and the canopy of a third, in excellent condition, forms a natural lath house for on-site nursery operations.

It is said that limbs of the oldest oaks here were used in the construction of Mission San Fernando, completed in 1797. The wood was not used, as you might expect, for massive exposed beams, nor for ordinary lumber. It was hauled, instead, to a kiln to be burned with limestone and so produce a powder for the mortar-making process. This accounts for the unusual shape of one venerable coast live oak; its lower branches cut off long ago, it is massively upright, not characteristically spreading.

Conservation of the Orcutt Ranch oaks remains a challenge, with problems typical to parks and gardens county wide:

oak root fungus, phytophthora crown rot, changes in watering patterns, and in this case, changes in fertilizing routine when orange trees were removed. (The oaks appear to have liked the extra nitrogen in the citrus trees' diet.) Two other widespread threats are the culverting of streams, which staunch Orcutt supporters prevented, and overzealous pruning, which it seems they did not.

William Orcutt's reputation was established when, exploring the La Brea tar pits for oil, he discovered the first skeletal remains of prehistoric animals, a curiosity and scientific resource for which the pits are now promoted. Orcutt constructed a spacious adobe house at Rancho Sombra del Roble in 1929. Colorful glazed tiles on its courtyard walls depict early Western life. Orcutt hired as gardener Ernest Carnejo, who abided with the ranch for fifty years. Carnejo's plant selections gave the property horticultural appeal and the planting design created subareas now variously favored for picnics, weddings, or cooling retreat. They are decorated by statuary, sundials, and suggestions of Indian culture, Mary Orcutt's interest.

Carnejo's eclectic tree palette includes lady palm (*Rhapis excelsa*), rattan palm (*R. humilis*), bunya-bunya (*Araucaria bidwillii*), cork oak (*Quercus suber*), and, in flower during our springtime visit, magnolias and the lace-mantled fringe tree (*Chionanthus virginicus*). In the formal rose garden, curved beds draw your eye to the pergola, a setting for marriage

ceremonies under the dome of the oak.

In the early years, citrus and walnut were planted extensively on the ranch. It appears that roughly half of the twenty-four extant acres remain in Valencia groves. Deeply furrowed, orderly rows hachure the property. Pendant orange globes gaily ornament the glossy foliage. The trees are watered with a very slow drip for a two-day period every six months. The public is invited to pick the fruit on a weekend announced for June or July. Proceeds pay for specialized garden tools beyond the basic city-allotted budget.

Oaks, oranges, and outreach. The third strength of Orcutt Ranch Horticulture Center is its system of community garden plots. A twenty-dollar yearly fee rents a ten-by-twenty-foot raised bed in full view of oranges, windmill, and the rust-red escarpment. Each plot is rototilled with redwood and compost, raked to final grade, and provided all the water the plants can drink. No harsh chemicals are allowed, and the only qualification for renters is enthusiasm. A patchwork of flowers and vegetables, the section is overseen by gardener Andy Morales, who is the personification of community service.

SHERMAN LIBRARY AND GARDENS

The Sherman Library and Gardens is modern, attractive, and neat as a pin. Any gardener aspiring to the good life in California will appreciate these interlocking outdoor rooms. Residential in scale, they are a fine assortment of spaces that can be covered in a pleasurable afternoon's time.

The Sherman Library and Gardens fills one city block in the comfortable seaside town of Corona del Mar. The library, tucked in a corner of the site, specializes in the Pacific Southwest, preserving as it does the papers of M. H. Sherman. Born in Vermont in 1853, Sherman chose Prescott, Arizona, at age twenty, then with a nose for rail transport came to Los Angeles at the turn of the century, where he formed and ultimately sold to Henry Huntington the Los Angeles Consolidated Electric Railway Company.

Directly behind the desk of veteran garden director Wade Roberts is a 1908 photograph of industrialist Sherman at the Bohemian Grove on the Russian River, the rustic retreat-cum-power-base of influential businessmen in Northern California. To his side, his right-hand man Arnold Haskell, who half a century later and entirely of his own volition would establish the Sherman Library and Gardens in his benefactor's memory. Haskell chose the site in Corona del Mar surrounding his own office, a tiny 1940s adobe cottage in the shade of a California pepper tree. The remainder of the block was gradually acquired for the Sherman Foundation.

Inspired by the rooftop tea garden at Derry and Tom's (later Biba's) Department Store in London, Haskell desired a garden of separate experiences and, in

addition, one that would serve the handicapped equally, a considerate notion decades ahead of its time, which has spared the Sherman the costly retrofit construction required of other public gardens.

There are several low buildings in the adobe tradition, but no central house to which the gardens report. Rather, the courtyards, tiled patios, greenhouses, and arbor-shaded walks form a sequence unto themselves and fit together smartly like a Rubic's cube. There is a breezy relationship between building and grounds, and an urbane use of paved surfaces within the garden matrix. Though different designers participated in garden planning over time, architect Nello Zava is characterized by Roberts as the one who "lived and breathed the project."

The horticultural goal at Sherman is to grant glorious color all year long. The Sun Garden and Central Garden, for example, feature bedding plants rotated by season; a springtime medallion of yolk-yellow marigolds, for example, where a scarlet carpet of poinsettias will be rolled out in December. The sources of animate color are diverse, as described below, but quantities are disciplined, a restraint that prevents the intimate gardens from feeling cluttered or cramped. At orderly Sherman, in a county known for conservatism, one would never expect a riot of color.

Permanent collections are nurtured for peak performance. In the Tropical Conservatory bloom orchids, vivid anthuriums, and variegated bromeliads. Dark green foliage half hides luminous koi gliding in a stone pool, an unexpected and pleasing display of this ubiquitous carp. The tuberous begonias in the Specimen Shade Garden erupt in late July and carry on until fall, a spectacular chromatic triangle of yellow, red, and white with every permutation on the palette in between: peach, salmon, orange, and pink.

Then there are the big terra-cotta pots and wall-hung planters with perennial showstoppers. No one can miss the *Brunfelsia pauciflora* mounted at eye level

on the white masonry wall outside the gift shop, its royal blue flowers set off by indigo stems. Or the pulsating mural of orchid cactus. Radiant red-hot reds and shocking pinks electrify the pepper tree patio from mid or late April into the first part of May.

There are flowering trees, but they are limited, as shade is the nemesis of many flowering shrubs and border plants. And finally, signature of the Tea Garden, there are the hanging baskets, swelling over with fuchsias and geraniums in the warmer tones of pastel pink and white to

suit the wedding ceremonies conducted here.

Tops among Sherman's foliage plants is the staggering herd of staghorn ferns flanking the grand entry. (In Southern California fashion, this ceremonial gateway gives on to the rear parking lot and not the main street of town.) There are two masterful garden structures worth special mention: the curving trellis that flows from the Tea Garden and, in the Discovery Garden, the refined two-tiered potting bench, which recounts in traditional clay containers a history of herbs in scent and touch for the blind, another legacy of the caring Mr. Haskell.

Gardens unerringly reflect environmental and cultural forces of the area in which they are found. That plant adaptation can be linked to geographical basics like climate and terrain is self-evident; that a public garden also mirrors cultural mores is undeniable at the Sherman Library and Gardens. Orange County is a prosperous region where wide streets and office blocks are neatly engineered, a brand new region whose transformation from fruited plain dates only from 1955, the year that Disneyland began, a well-dressed region whose meeting place is South Coast Plaza, the busiest shopping mall in the country. And so we find a well-furbished garden, conceived in 1958, that is a handsome contemporary design, manicured to the point of make believe in this era of diminished maintenance resources, and as savvy as a retail display with its eye-catching show of color. In fact, despite its affluent air, the Sherman Library and Gardens must compete head-on with the countless recreational pursuits in Orange County to engage the general public.

BALBOA PARK

When San Diego's population numbered a scant two thousand, in 1868, an astonishing fourteen hundred acres were set aside for a city park. Then, in a fever of hoopla and boosterism in 1909, the park's central mesa was transformed. An exposition planned to coincide with the opening of the Panama Canal would advertise San Diego as the first U.S. port of call for ships heading north from the passage. In a clever tie-in, the park where the fair would be held was renamed for the explorer Balboa, who crossed the Isthmus of Panama and happened upon the Pacific Ocean.

The 1915 Panama-California Exposition adopted a Spanish Colonial theme, and the florid buildings that occupy the central portion of Balboa Park today are holdovers from that exuberant event, as are many fine civic spaces between buildings. To proclaim the gentle climate, the exposition was landscaped to a fare-thee-well. Two million plants were set out, many of them large trees and shrubs transplanted from private homes, and so it was dubbed the Garden Fair.

According to historian Gregory Montes, an erstwhile plan that would have better preserved the natural character of the park was prepared by the eminent landscape architectural firm Olmsted Brothers, of Brookline, Massachusetts. On a hill toward the south end of Balboa Park, John Olmsted designed a formal avenue flanked by arcaded sidewalks with gardens, waterfalls, and pavilions nestled in a canyon to one side. But real estate interests, insensitive to encroachment upon the middle of Balboa Park, forced the relocation of the fairgrounds there, ostensibly to meet the requirements of exhibitors, but all the while banking on an

extension of a streetcar from the central site that would serve their suburban property holdings.

The encrusted, picturesque architecture is the work of Bertram G. Goodhue, a self-described "shark" when it came to historicist styles, particularly the one at hand. Goodhue wrested the commission from local favorite Irving Gill, who practiced the more restrained Mission style, by referring the selection committee to a ten-volume work about the Spanish Colonial architecture of Mexico illustrated by none other than the shark himself. Eager to distinguish the San Diego effort from the competing Panama-Pacific International Exposition in San Francisco, a classical design in the Beaux Arts manner, the feisty San Diego organizers embraced Goodhue's ornate imagery. The creation of fanciful but fully realized environments seems to be a local specialty, from the whimsical worlds of San Diegan Dr. Seuss to the downtown shopping mall Horton Plaza, a vividly colorful stage set of an Italian piazza.

At the time the Botanical Building was erected it was the largest structure of its type in the world, approaching in scale the famous conservatory at Kew Gardens and reminiscent of it in general shape and purpose. The Balboa Park version relies on San Diego's mild temperatures, substituting miles of redwood lath for glass over its arching steel framework. It resembles more closely the sprawling Huntington Botanical Gardens lath

house, now demolished, although a more compact edition. Under the central dome, umbrellalike spokes permit an unimpeded span of seventy-five feet and the cultivation of ascending palm trees. A 1915 photograph looks not unlike the inside of the Botanical Building today, a leafy netherworld that defies definition as indoors or out: feathery Australian tree ferns (*Alsophila australis*), split-leaf philodendron (*Monstera deliciosa 'Ceriman'*), and staghorn ferns mounted on wall-hung plaques like hunting trophies in a baronial hall.

The Botanical Building is most important as enclosure and focal point for the garden called La Laguna. This is the finest of a series of spaces off El Prado, the grand promenade and organizational spine of the exposition plan, which culminates in a white plume of water against the blue sky. The lagoon is a long, rectangular pool. Its dark waters, planted sparely to water lilies and hypnotic yellow lotus, reflect the even pattern of slats and staves, an effect also similar to Kew. An arched, stucco entry grounds the airy lath house and allies it with nearby buildings, notably an elegant arcade of paired columns that it confronts across El Prado.

The Alcazar Garden, down the promenade, disappointed me at first, being a copy of only a small portion of the intricate complex of famous gardens in Seville. Palace to the Moorish kings, the original Alcazar was sacked by the Spanish in 1248 and rebuilt by them a century later, employing Moors as craftsmen and laborers. Charles V later added Renaissance elements, and it is from his courtyards that the Balboa Park tableau derives. Compartmentalized by walls and tall hedges, the patios and gardens of the Seville Alcazar are memorable for details of tile and masonry and, above all, the refreshing sound of water. Fountains are ubiquitous though mostly modest affairs, sunk into the path without coping. Window seats are set into thick walls, with grills providing glimpses of adjoining gardens. Benches, fountains, stair risers, and much else are covered by *azulejos*, colorful glazed tiles with lively abstract patterns. (Muslim law prohibited the representation of people or animals.) Unglazed terra-cotta pavers or black-and-white pebble mosaics make a simple but sensual walking surface. There are

tall palms, clipped hedges, and an economical use of water for plantings.

At Balboa's Alcazar, I found that walking on scored concrete tinted red, between dwarfed rows of boxwood and toward a silent fountain, did not carry me to far-off Spain. But departing through the arcade defining one side of the garden, a Depression-era addition for a revival exposition, the view from the deep shade back to the bright courtyard changed my opinion. Through arches rendered with elegant restraint in concrete, the fountains, greenery, baroque portals, and polychrome decoration proved, at a slight but forgiving distance, an evocative if not impeccable combination after all.

As you tour Balboa Park, the finest old trees that catch your eye are the legacy of Kate Olivia Sessions, a dedicated horticulturist who altered gardening habits by popularizing native and imported species. (Matilija poppy, Mexican flannel bush, and lemon-scented and red-flowering eucalyptus were among her favorites.) In 1892, she was permitted thirty acres of the city's central park for an experimental nursery in exchange for annually planting "100 choice and varied sorts of trees" in the park and furnishing "300 ornamental trees in crocks or boxes" for street and school-yard beautification. For twelve years, the public beat a path to her door, and so Balboa Park developed both an early following and a landscape framework. Look for cork oak, camphor tree, queen palm, and

Brandagee palm (*Brahea brandegeei*). Sessions collected the Brandagee palm seed on a trip to Cabo San Lucas with the naturalist after whom the species was named.

Other horticultural destinations in Balboa Park are garden types represented throughout Southern California: collections of roses, gardenias, camellias, and cacti; the Palm Canyon, another Garden Fair descendant; and soon a Japanese Friendship Garden. But nowhere else will you find the likes of the remarkable but rarely acclaimed botanical garden called the San Diego Zoo.

It is a separate entity within Balboa Park, and as implied by an asphalt parking lot vast enough to serve a major league stadium, the attendance is phenomenal: every year 3.75 million people visit this garden. It also happens to be a zoo.

The San Diego Zoo is recognized for its engaging, ecological approach. Lavish habitats show how various forms of plant and animal life are integrated within particular bioclimates, say the tropical rain forest. Here is the opposite of the "This is a gorilla" method of the old zoo school. Cleverly staged, walk-through exhibits are intensely landscaped to approximate a natural environment both for the creatures' well-being and because animals are more highly valued in the proper context. An enormous variety of robust trees, shrubs, and vines are deftly arranged to serve the purpose, but of equal importance the greenery has a subtle yet powerful influence. Unbeknownst to the viewer, it is the plants, not the wildlife, which are conducive to an exceptional zoo experience.

The hundred-acre site offers a variety of landforms inviting showmanship and changes in level. Benign microclimates broaden the horticultural palette ("Exotic plants are more powerful, they draw people closer," explained horticulturist Chuck Coburn, as always imbuing botany with philosophy) and increase the possibility of accurate and nutritional selections for the inhabitants. Enterprising keepers who understood herbology for animals were the first to gather landscape clippings to use as feed; now browsing is a regular staff duty. The koala, for example, regulates its metabolism by eating different kinds of eucalyptus. There had been instances at other zoos when elephants were fed packages of marshmallows, carton and all.

There is a playfulness to the horticultural design here, a joyful creativity that is as pleasurable to the visitor as beauty and ecological balance. Cloudbursts of mist humidify plants along the jungly path of Tiger River, helping the

rest of us to a welcome facial. Irrigation line twines through the canopy like a liana to water treetop epiphytes. Twigs, rocks, and soil have been pressed into Gunite surface for an artistic rendition of dirt. At the commercial nursery, misshapen plants rejected by others are seized upon for their character, the more irregular the better. And with moxie burly figs are moved from one part of the zoo to another. "There is only one way to transplant megatrees," Coburn told me with a smile: "Root a toot toot!"

The San Diego Zoo is seeking accreditation as a botanic garden, which will increase recognition for its uninhibited ways and considerable collections, among them gingers, orchids, coral trees, and cycads. But it will not alter expectations regarding the public's response to the plants. "If someone says 'I learned fifty new species today,' that won't make me happy," Coburn explained, citing the primacy of the human experience over the botanical one. Thus, the tram queue forms on an elevated boardwalk wending through a tree canopy, a considerate (and educational) way to derail impatience in line. The tour bus travels a service road enclosed by a slope so densely covered with subtropical vegetation that it could be mistaken for the interior of Panama, a thoughtful interlude for the riders en route to eagerly awaited animal displays. It was there that I saw the papery brown rosette of the banana tree flower for the first time. Yet the botanical richness is often taken for granted. As a befuddled

tourist whispered audibly when my husband paused for a photograph on the luxuriant path somewhere between the tapir and the fishing cat, in the new three-acre rain forest, "Why is he taking a picture of a plant?"

As a garden, the San Diego Zoo is singularly animated by frequent encounters with magnificent wild creatures and the awe they inspire in us. Nonetheless, it was a relief for us to divest ourselves from the knots of jostling onlookers at the animal attractions and, unimpeded, take in the plant life that makes the day.

SPECIAL

PURPOSE

GARDENS

THE J. PAUL GETTY MUSEUM

MALIBU

On the Bay of Naples, in the village of Resina, a peasant deepening his well in 1709 uncovered to his amazement several fragments of colored marble. The marble turned out to be part of an upper tier of seats in a theater and the theater part of an entire city, buried in 65 feet of solidified ash. Herculaneum, a seaside resort for wealthy Romans, had not been seen since the tumultuous eruption of Mount Vesuvius in A.D. 79. Fishermen's dwellings and farmers' fields were sitting directly on top of it, and that incidental discovery instigated a subterranean treasure hunt that lasted fifty years before collapsing foundations and the seepage of poisonous gas made it impossible to continue.

In 1738, the sticky-fingered Spanish Bourbon king of Naples, Charles III, enlarged the scope of the operations and claimed their spoils as his alone. The finds at Herculaneum and neighboring Pompeii had sparked a continental rage for things classical, but both scholars and the merely curious were denied entry to his collection, or if granted visitation, proscribed from sketching.

Burrowing went on for more than a decade with booty the only objective, until a methodical Swiss engineer, Karl Weber, was put in charge in 1750. Unlike archaeological digs in which layers of history are unpeeled from the top down, the search for Herculaneum was by mole's route. Slowly chipping away at volcanic rock, an elaborate system of shored up tunnels and passageways was eked underground. Weber's predecessor had been so single-minded about pirating that many objects considered less than perfect as artworks had been disposed of. Callously he had pried bronze letters from ancient walls without first recording the

inscription. Weber, for his part, being painstaking instead of greedy, ran afoul of his superiors, but thanks to his patient record keeping and draftsmanship we can stroll the peristyle of a splendid "country villa" in Malibu, its provenance coastal Italy before the common era.

A peristyle is a colonnade enclosing an outdoor space, but the word alone does not adequately describe the two-thousand-year-old presence of the museum's long, rectangular garden court. It is an exquisite three-dimensional composition. At one end, against a backdrop of trees and open hillside, the magisterial villa; at the other, the Corinthian columns of an open portico frame lithe sycamores and glimpses of the blue Pacific. On either side of the central court, white Doric columns pace a covered walkway. For every fluted shaft, a graphic band of mosaic—black, white, and tan in a Greek key—segments the polished red terrazzo floor, with geometric medallions striking the downbeat every second bay. The inner walls are frescoed with swag garlands suspended between trompe l'oeil columns, in a palette of yellow ochre, terra-cotta,

white, and gray-green that glows in the reflected light of garden and pool. The painted surfaces are pierced by grilles with views to the landscape beyond. (Isolation from intrusive contemporary views is one reason this site is so keenly suited to its purpose.) It is a slow and sumptuous walk down the peristyle to the villa, a dramatic first act to the fabled collections at the J. Paul Getty Museum.

The garden court is formal and symmetrical. Boxwood and bay laurel standards, clipped into precise forms, seem as architectural as column and pediment, their solid, glossy greens an effective foil to the matte reds, yellows, and whites of the surrounding structure. All lines are clean—the paths, the grape arbor, the sturdy marble plinths—and everything is impeccably groomed. Yet in spite of its orderliness and reserve, this remarkable outdoor room is in motion. The low boxwood hedges swerve into semicircles around each bay tree. Paving spins in radial patterns. Startled white eyes in dark bronze busts watch as you go by, and the surface of the long central pool, a pale wash of aquamarine, the color of warm sea shallows, is rippled by fount and breeze. When the coastal fog burns away, light dances off the water and knows no boundaries. Even the gilt ceiling rosettes in their coffered recesses are illuminated. At each end of the pool, sculpted figures appreciate this setting in expressive ways: one faun reclines languorously in the sun, the other reaches upward with intoxicated joy.

Why is the peristyle garden so powerful? It looks so different from what we are accustomed to, but it speaks to us directly. We may not know the vocabulary, but we sense deeply what it says. This is the heritage of Western civilization. This is the lineage of many great public spaces that compose our frame of reference. The peristyle is well rendered surely, and the materials surpass expectations, but more than quality is at work on our psyche here. In the classical school, there were rules that governed size, proportion, spacing, and favored combinations, a regulated framework that even today unleashes compositions guaranteed to please the eye. Ultimately, the peristyle garden speaks to us because it is beautiful. The buildings, water, sculpture, and usable spaces are brought together in a rich and satisfying format so unlike the homogenized gruel of modern development.

This is a likeness of the Villa dei Papiri, named for the crumbling papyrus scrolls unearthed in its Greek library. For more than two centuries, this villa was the country retreat of harried Roman aristocrats seeking respite from long days of political intrigue at the Forum, about two hundred kilometers away. With the security of empire and with leisure time assured by a brutal system of slavery, Roman taste became refined in artistic spheres. A residential style evolved in Pompeii and Herculaneum for the *villa suburbana,* an atrium house responsive to the Mediterranean climate. Private

rooms were arranged around an open-roofed court where guests were received and business conducted. As the atrium house became more elaborate, walled gardens to the rear were replaced by Greek peristyles, and rooms for dining, sleeping, and bathing surrounded the new, inner colonnade. The Romans used their gardens extensively for work and pleasure. The atrium itself receded in importance and functioned more like an entry hall.

The J. Paul Getty Museum is a harmonious approximation (drawing liberally on other villas for inspiration when evidence did not exist) of the Villa dei Papiri after it had been "improved" in the first century B.C., but even by Roman standards this was no ordinary house addition. A second peristyle was added, 310 feet long by 104 feet wide, with a file of 65 columns on its seaward portico, and in the center a deep pool, 218 feet long by 24 feet wide, bigger than some public baths in Rome. What a retreat: architecture, gardens and sculpture, friends, fresh produce and regional wine, summer reading, lap swimming, servants, and the sea, all to meet a sudden cataclysmic end with the fiery explosion of Mount Vesuvius.

J.P. Getty had a passion for things classical, and he possessed unlimited means to indulge. Suffice it to say that even among oil men, he was in a league of his own; today the J. Paul Getty Trust and its wealth of programs are the envy of world-class museums. By 1955, in addition to amassing antiquities, Getty had

written a historical novella. The action transpires at the original Villa dei Papiri, where Glaucus, the landscape architect, is hero and his Roman patron bears a striking resemblance to author Getty himself.

Getty's reconstruction in the Santa Monica Mountains of the patrician residence that so intrigued him shows the same enterprising determination illustrated in his autobiography, *As I See It*. As a young man in Los Angeles, he regularly rolled his father's Chadwick out of the garage and down the hill to jump start it for late-night forays, until the time he found the wheels chained to the cement floor, wine stains having been detected on the upholstery. J.P. turned around and built his own car, a low-slung two-seater with a Lincoln engine, to which he attached the rakish moniker "Plaza Milano," and he was off again. At Malibu, when the art collection outgrew its quarters, Getty turned around and built his own Villa dei Papiri next door. It opened in 1974.

Plant selection was a matter of well-educated guesswork. Myrtle, bay, rose, and oleander are among plants documented in written accounts. Frescoes preserved from Pompeii and Herculaneum informed the plan with *Viburnum tinus* and ivy trained in balls on wire cages. Inside one of these ivy cages in the inner peristyle is an Oregon junco nest, an example of the wildlife in these gardens, also represented in the frescoes by Garth Benton. Study Benton's festoons, then look for the same species in

the gardens: white madonna lilies, scarlet anemone, poet's narcissus, campanula, violas, pansies, and the red-and-white-striped clusiana tulip; plum, peach, and cherry; apple, grape, and pomegranate. Many of these are found in the herb garden, a wonderfully unfettered counterpart to the peristyles.

There is color in the herb garden and the scent of aromatic leaves. Plants were of fundamental importance to Roman civilization, depended upon as larder, pharmacy, ritual offering, and raw material, and in these plots the imaginative exploration of ancient breeds is given free reign: single-grain wheat (*Triticum monococcum*), broccoli (they ate the big leaves, not the tiny florets), safflower, yarrow, lovage, mullein, and mint (we tasted three types). There is a chrysanthemum (*C. balsamita*) that placed in books discourages silverfish, and another (*C. cinerariifolium*) whose dried petals are a natural source of the insecticide pyrethrum, which the Getty gardeners harvest for that purpose. Flax (*Linum usitatissimum*) is the plant that launched a thousand ships: from its stem fibers came linen for sails; from the oil of its seed, a

wood finish still common today. Fig trees, olives, date palms, and stone pine are so evocative of the ancient Mediterranean that you can ignore the large, essentially blank outer wall of the peristyle.

In Italy, soil scanning with electron microscopes, carbon dating of olive remains, and castings poured into root cavities have added to the knowledge of appropriate species. Then there are horticultural rules of thumb: use pure strains, not hybrids, or let hybrids return to their parent form, like the larkspur that willingly reverted to seven-foot-tall spikes of long-lasting purple bloom.

The gardening staff at the Getty contends with the unlikeness of conditions in southern Italy and Southern California. Malibu can be very foggy, and this leads to mildew and other cultural problems. (Hence the Japanese box instead of English box, a Mediterranean native, in the main garden court.) What now is the herb garden was at the beginning an impenetrable, compacted backfill that had to be dug up with jackhammers; the east garden soil was replaced altogether. In contrast, the soil in the peristyle is lightweight (as is necessitated for roof gardens like this one, which sits on a parking garage) but infertile. In Herculaneum, pumice, ash, and organic matter made for soil and drainage that were "just beautiful! They could grow anything there," said assistant grounds superintendent Steve Cutting with plantsman's envy.

The inner peristyle is similar in its use of greenery, water, and statuary to the grand garden on the other side of the vestibule, but it is an intimate, conversational space. Cutting tells me with satisfaction that frequently, while he is working in here, a tourist who has escaped the gallery atmosphere will come up to him and confide, "This is for me. I like it much better outside."

Beginning with the Italian Renaissance, there have been periodic and influential revivals of classical arts and architecture. Today there is a new creative circle whose members find relevance in classical forms. They do not pursue postmodernism; indeed they react against that genre's often impoverished forms. If the Getty Museum has stimulated your taste, I recommend *Classical Architecture: Rule and Invention,* by architect Thomas Gordon Smith, practitioner of a vibrant contemporary classicism.

EXPOSITION PARK ROSE GARDEN

LOS ANGELES

Roses are a convivial lot, greeted everywhere as friends, for who doesn't know the rose by name? Willingly, the likable rose bonds with any passerby who consents to the sweet intimacy of a sniff.

In every crowd, of course, there is always someone whose taste tends to clean lines and unadorned white walls, an adherent to Modern design who finds roses too ornamental; the bushes too cluttered with flowers; the plants too effusive in their charms. But even the sanctimonious would find satisfaction at Exposition Park, because architecturally the layout of the rose garden is so crisp and strong.

Broad grass walkways firmly edged with white concrete bands define two hundred, mostly rectangular rose beds, each filled with plants of a single cultivar. The green field, the long white lines, the uniform beds display sheer color more effectively than other rose gardens I've seen: the lustrous red velvet of 'Olympiad,' the outspoken orange of 'Shreveport,' the metallic lavender of 'Sterling Silver,' the trilogy—pink, red and white—of 'Global Delight.'

It is called a sunken garden, this seven-and-a-half-acre plain. An enormous rectangle, it is set below grade about three feet, although relative to the scale of the flat expanse, the change in level is quite subtle from within. In the center is a circular fountain with jets and lights (although these have been inoperative for many years).

The Spanish Renaissance facade of the Museum of Natural History (architects Hudson and Munsell, 1912) encloses the far end of the garden, its dome and arches providing a focal point in the classical tradition to terminate the long garden axis. The formal entrance to the garden is on the cross-axis, flanked by pillars inscribed to remind us that as stars are the poetry of heaven, flowers are the poetry of the earth, but for anyone who has caught the wafting bouquet or glimpsed the spectacular show here, no reminder is needed. The corners of the sunken garden are rounded and framed

by the deep green of conifers, and the entire perimeter is described by an aging brick balustrade with cast stone cap, a perfect perch from which to watch the goings-on below.

There are Sundays at Exposition Park Rose Garden, when the four white pergolas are booked for simultaneous weddings, that the beautiful young women in fluttering pastel layers of satin and chiffon from the various processions look like animated roses escaped from the planting beds. One party is the blushing pink of 'Sheer Bliss' come to life; another the sunny yellow of 'Gold Medal.' Gingerly making their way in high heels on the turf, the maids' colorful regalia is set off by the soft green walkways much as the roses are. What a place to be seen.

There is a lively Hispanic flavor here that adds to the festive atmosphere. *"Vamanos al quiosco!"* a tuxedo-clad usher calls, hurrying toward the arbor, while more casually attired Chicanos scrutinize the action or buy *paletas* from a pushcart before the vendor of these frozen treats, who is performing a public service, is chased off by the patrolman on beat. For residents of cramped quarters in nearby neighborhoods, the Rose Garden has become a proper place to gather and promenade, fulfilling the purpose of the grand civic quadrangle that predated the installation of fifteen thousand roses, in 1926–27.

Orlando Alayu, head gardener at the Exposition Park Rose Garden, recom-

mends visiting between June and September for peak bloom, although the flowering period extends from the last of April to early November. The collection includes hybrid teas, grandifloras, miniature roses, and climbers, all of which replace the original plants. Alayu revealed a five-point program for successful rose culture: patience, work, daily inspection of every bed, a little education, and well-timed pest control. (Weary amateurs who have had skirmishes with aphids and spider mites, mildew and rust would simplify this to a one-point program, the last.)

Alayu told me he enjoys talking to visitors, especially the occasional old-timer who came here as a child. I've heard that before, was my silent reaction, but later realized with chagrin that I hadn't. Hardly another public garden in Los Angeles is this old. Some were in existence in the twenties but were as yet personal estates or ranches; a few places of botanic interest went back seventy years, but they were parks or private property.

Despite this heritage, there have been schemes concocted to undo the garden, which is leased by the city of Los Angeles from the state, which in turn owns most of Exposition Park. One scheme proposed a multilevel underground parking garage with the roses "transplanted" to the roof; another sought without remorse to clear the quad and make it a practice field for the newly arrived Raiders football team. In reaction, the Exposition

Park Rose Garden was designated a Los Angeles County landmark and put under consideration for listing in the National Register of Historic Places.

For more than a century the rose has been prominent in the Southern California landscape. Its history goes back to the missions, and by 1880, according to Victoria Padilla's account in *Southern California Gardens,* the roses of Southern California were astounding newcomers with their profusion and practically perpetual display. That same year Lucky Baldwin of the Rancho Santa Anita (now the Los Angeles State and County Arboretum) sent to France for rose bushes and an expert in *parfumerie* to accompany them, in an optimistic and typically Victorian effort to launch a perfume industry here. Owing, however, to the dryness of the San Gabriel Valley, which inhibited the natural production of scented oil, the experiment failed.

During the 1940s and 1950s, Southern California became extremely important in the arena of rose hybridization, being the most productive region in the world in the development of new varieties of exceptional quality. And that, ultimately, is the point. This is not just a good or even very good municipal rose garden. The rose is the world's most popular flower and this is the foremost rose garden in the home of American rose breeding.

SELF-REALIZATION FELLOWSHIP LAKE SHRINE

Here is a placid retreat where plants and landscape design are in service to a higher purpose. The greenery and natural forms are a means, not an end, the tranquil setting pretty but secondary to the act of meditation it sustains.

The ten-acre Self-Realization Fellowship Lake Shrine is an open-air temple and features the first memorial in the world to Mahatma Gandhi, the charismatic religious leader who won freedom for India through a doctrine of non-violence. The property is located in a bowl of the Santa Monica Mountains, within reach of salty off-shore breezes and surrounding a spring-fed lake that fills a former rock quarry. The Gandhi World Peace Memorial is one of several "stops" on a circular lakeside walk, a gently graded fir-bark path that is pleasantly landscaped and discreetly accompanied by plaques with diverse theological quotations — from Psalms, the New Tes-

tament, and other sources, the shrine being dedicated to all religions — or with the polite but secular admonition "No reclining on grass, please."

The memorial's Golden Lotus Archway is no more than the simplest diagram of a structure, its white posts and beams crowned by iconographic, gilt lotus blossoms, symbols of the soul, the whole shining composition in effective relief against the verdant backdrop of hillside vegetation. Through the portal, at the rear of the small grassy court, is an

He who perceives Me everywhere,
and beholds everything in Me,
never loses sight of Me, nor
do I ever lose sight of him.
BG VI:30

ancient, reverential Chinese sarcophagus, flanked by two diminutive marble statues of Kwan Yin, the Chinese Goddess of Mercy. Here lies a portion of Gandhi's ashes.

Gandhi and Paramahansa Yogananda, founder of the Self-Realization Fellowship, had a union of spirit, the Mahatma in 1935 having requested initiation in Kriya Yoga, Yogananda's technique for meditation. The Self-Realization Fellowship Lake Shrine opened in 1950, two years after Gandhi's assassination. Paramahansa Yogananda is known outside the fold for his life account, *Autobiography of a Yogi,* which is dedicated to Luther Burbank, although any posthumous influence by Burbank on Yogananda's decision to merge plant life with spiritual quest in this unwalled temple is not recorded. According to lore within the Fellowship, the yogi directed placement of plants on shore from a small boat floating in the center of the lake.

There is indeed a contemplative hush at the shrine and a welcome exclusion of the world at large. "When people first arrive, they are really restless," observed fellowship gardener Jack Hudkins, "but by the time they get about halfway around the lake, they are calm." This is due in part to the enveloping topography and also to the soothing effect of water. To some, however, the juxtaposition of Dutch windmill, Mississippi riverboat, swaying palms, and several swans-a-swimming is more playful than peaceful. All are in full view from most points along the walk.

The feature that distinguishes the Self-Realization Fellowship Lake Shrine among public gardens is the large selection of highly personal places to sit. While most gardens provide benches, none accommodates pause in as liberal a fashion as this and some even prohibit reflection, their docents charged with chaperoning the hapless visitor at all times. But here, just off the path, are numerous sanctioned spots. No two are alike, each a small and individualized space with a short bench. If other places have garden rooms, then in the monastic sense these must be garden cells. One is a shaded nook within earshot of a rushing waterfall; another a sunny, wooden dock; a third, a tiny terrace secretly nestled above the walk; a fourth the domed fern grotto near the museum; and so on. Surely the repeat visitor strengthens a mental claim to a favored corner on every return.

FRANKLIN D. MURPHY
SCULPTURE GARDEN, UCLA

WESTWOOD

This is a well-loved garden, although it lacks many conventional garden elements. It is gateless, with a loosely defined perimeter and just a simple palette of plants. The space flows and the eye wanders at will. The students who use the courtyard for study or relaxation stroll equally unimpeded until they settle upon a grassy mound or inside a concrete seat wall. Nor is the sculpture confined: it is encountered on the terraces, patios, and campus walks adjoining the central courtyard. The curve and swell of the site plan exemplify a modern landscape architectural motif that originated in California. The open, free-form design is collegial to the twentieth-century artwork and complements it.

Pilotis elevate the base of Ralph Bunche Hall, creating a passageway two stories high to the Franklin D. Murphy Sculpture Garden. Pilotis are flattened concrete piers, in the manner of Le Corbusier, an architectural spokesman of the Modern Movement. As used here, the slender, tapering rectangles (with a crease on their presenting end) serve as portal to the sculpture court. The clean geometry of other, surrounding buildings, dedicated primarily to the visual and performing arts, maintains the contemporary setting, as do broad bands of shallow steps that accomplish changes in grade.

There are more than fifty works of art representing the era's foremost sculptors, including Auguste Rodin, Henry Moore, Alexander Calder, Jean Arp, and Aristide Maillol. Figurative, abstract, or constructivist, they make a diverse yet egalitarian assemblage, with no piece placed more prominently than another. The layout is gracious, more akin to a small park than a museum, and is decidedly unlike the acclaimed but cramped and rigid sculpture garden at the Norton Simon Museum in Pasadena. Here at UCLA there are untold numbers of

vantage points and combinations. Bronze, stone, steel, and stainless steel are viewed against the softer surfaces of foliage and lawn on approximately five acres. Among personal favorites of mine on a recent visit were the imperious female torso by Gaston Lachaise (1932) and in their yogic strength and balance, Dance Columns I and II, by Robert Graham (1978).

One night at a landscape architects' banquet in San Francisco, a guest at our table responded to the inevitable question, "A sculptor." Skeptical of the claim, I was convinced of his talent and vocation when he demonstrated professional understanding of materials. A headache-inducing spotlight assaulted our eyes during the awards presentation. Only he, of all the squinting party guests, took the evening's printed program and with two deft tears and some folding produced a serviceable visor. Smugly tilted back in his chair, he watched the rest of the show in comfort. For UCLA students, the three-dimensionality of sculpture is in tangible contrast to ideas and paper all day long. How restorative it must be to move from the flatness of note pad and printout to the carved, cut, cast, and constructed forms of sculpture — outstanding sculpture, in quantity, and in the landscape.

Most people associate the Franklin D. Murphy Sculpture Garden with the Brazilian jacaranda tree (*Jacaranda mimosifolia*), the garden's concession to flowering interest. In late spring or early summer, eight-inch-long clusters of

blossoms cast an enchanting lavender veil across the leafless branches. Yet more spectacular, but not for their deep red-orange winter bloom, is the double and, for a stretch, triple row of mature coral trees (*Erythrina caffra*) along the north side of the garden, in front of MacGowan Hall. In retort to the pilotis on the south side, they frame tunnellike views with multiple trunks as kinetic and muscular as any torso sculpture on the grounds. Under the dim coral tree arcade the deep bronze-green color of figurative pieces seems more skinlike than similar work in the open, where highlights tend to pick out a metallic sheen.

The garden was designed by the late Ralph Cornell, principal landscape architect for the Westwood campus for thirty-five years and a widely accomplished practitioner in Southern California. It was the inspiration of Chancellor Franklin D. Murphy, advocate of art in the lives of young men and women and protector of the parklike character of the campus. In the early 1960s he envisioned, where a dusty parking lot stood, students talking, reading, holding classes, and enjoying the collaboration of nature and art in a sculpture garden. Today they pose unconsciously, fulfilling that ambition.

JAPANESE

GARDENS

THE UCLA HANNAH CARTER JAPANESE GARDEN

BEL AIR

The enjoyment of most gardens is an involuntary response to sensual stimuli—the warmth of the sun and the coolness of greenery, the scent of flowers, the flagrant color of bloom, and so on. In a Japanese garden, the pleasure can be as simple and intuitive as that, but the intentions are more complex, and an understanding of the conventions permits fuller appreciation.

In Japanese garden art, metaphor and literary allusion play a critical role. Large-scale scenic features, like a mountain or forest, are represented in the medium of plants, stone, or water. Furthermore, fragments of scenes from literature, like *The Tale of the Genji,* are reproduced in the garden setting. A cultured Japanese responds to these resonant symbols as automatically as the uninitiated would swoon over a mantle of cherry blossoms or a bonfire of autumn color. A pool, for example, represents the sea, which is highly revered by this island nation, and

the crescent of smooth gray cobbles secured at the water's edge suggests the shore. There goes a tale of a commoner who presented to the emperor a selection of perfect cobbles each wrapped in silk, only to be driven to suicide by his shogun for breaching a ban on offerings to royalty. To the well-informed, then, the symbolic beach can also be a subtle reminder of social proscriptions.

The UCLA Hannah Carter Japanese Garden is a compendium of Japanese garden features and designs. Landscape architect Nagao Sakurai drew from the city of Kyoto, bastion of Japanese culture, where more than fifty gardens in good condition remain from

its thousand-year reign as the Imperial City. The entry gate, for example, is in the style of the Ichida Estate in that ancient capital. A tile-roofed, white plastered wall, with projecting wings defining the threshold, it is a handsome landmark carefully inset in a crook of Bellagio Road. The gate structure becomes a picture frame when the door of sacred cryptomeria wood swings open, revealing a glimpse of illuminated green, a perfect Zen view.

Behind the gate rises a lush and densely planted hillside, graced with bird song and a canopy of coast live oak. The plan applies the Kyoto tradition of hide-and-reveal: as the path climbs, twists, and turns, vignettes are screened, made manifest, then abruptly removed from view. There are no axes here, no focal points in the Western manner. Asymmetry, naturalness, and the subtlety of seasons prevail.

In 1965, Edward W. Carter, chairman of the state Board of Regents, donated to UCLA the Japanese Garden that the Gordon Guiberson family had completed in 1961. The plan is an ingenious adaptation of Japanese themes to the vertical topography of Bel Air. The central element is a stream that courses melodically downhill. Odd numbers are common in Japanese gardens, especially the number three, and here are found the three states of water: flowing, cascading, and still. Moreover, the water is a stage for other garden prototypes: the zigzag stepping stones that defy evil spirits to pass; the wild boar-scarer, or in this case raccoon-scarer, a bamboo tube that self-fills with water, then tips with a sudden, hollow knock; the "turtle" stone brought from the rapids of the Hozu River near Kyoto; three millstones; the glittering koi.

In addition, the UCLA Hannah Carter Japanese Garden is a veritable museum of garden artifacts, all transported from Japan—Buddha carvings, stone water basins, five-tiered pagoda, lanterns, Chinese lions, and more. In Japan, ornament in gardens is applied more sparely than in many American versions, where the stone art seems to be used by the shipload.

The Japanese have a fondness for shaping plants. Their practice of bonsai for miniature trees is widely known. Another pruning technique, called *karikami*, the clipping of hedges to symbolize other landscape features (say boulders, waves, or foothills) can be seen at

the UCLA Japanese Garden, though they are not as refined in execution as are paragons in Japan. Azalea bushes (kurume and indica types) are sculpted into spheres as at the garden at Shisen-do, a technique that maximizes both the quantity and drama of the bloom in March. The effect is of an ardent collector's display of Venetian glass paperweights. It is resplendent, but differs from the true Japanese in two respects: at Shisen-do, flowers are removed to rein in the intensity of color, and the clipped shrubs are more uniform and globelike.

"Authenticity!" is the battle cry of Japanese garden experts in California, but can that fervent goal be achieved on foreign soil? Can the atmosphere and mystical mood of Kyoto with its stifling, humid summers and chilling winters be replicated in dry and genial Southern California under strong Mediterranean light? Climatically, Georgia might prove more fitting, but lacking still would be the context of cultural wealth beyond the garden walls.

For a close approximation, like this garden, a Japanese landscape designer can be engaged who knows the philosophical signposts. Antiquities and rocks can be imported. Major structures like the teahouse and family shrine can be built in Japan, then reassembled here by native artisans. And above all, the craftsmanship of garden installation must excel. The Japanese are meticulous in traditional construction, with their arse-

nal of precision-made hand tools, a penchant for fine-grained and fragrant wood, and a religious adherence to the simple and pure.

Finally there is the matter of perception. In a Japanese garden the act of comprehending the metaphor and allusion is as much a part of the garden as the leaning pines. The presence of people who understand what they see is the grace note of authenticity, a note that can echo in a foreign land but never ring clear.

It may not matter. A Japanese garden holds such enormous appeal as an art form and place of tranquility that Californians seem willingly to forgo the fine points for an opportunity to enter the exotic Orient and partake at any level. The shorthand of poodle-cut junipers and mass-produced concrete lanterns adrift in lava rock can be seen in countless residential yards. The UCLA Hannah Carter Japanese Garden emerged from the same fascination, but represents the scholarly end of the spectrum.

EARL BURNS MILLER JAPANESE GARDEN

LONG BEACH

Alumni day at Cal State Long Beach, and the Earl Burns Miller Japanese Garden was hopping. It seemed as if every couple who had met on campus was returning to their trysting place only to encounter dozens of other nostalgic graduates doing the same. The student monitor, accustomed to sanctity within this jade green retreat, was besieged: people perched themselves on sacred rocks; excited children stampeded the zigzag bridge. There was an atmosphere of gaiety alien to a Japanese garden, but not entirely unbecoming. Here was proof that composition and verdure can give pleasure directly, irrespective of symbolism.

The Earl Burns Miller Japanese garden has traditional components—teahouse, stone lanterns, azalea, iris, and pine—and it is distinguished by the sympathetic grace with which the elements have been combined. The approach to the one-acre garden is offset, so that the visitor is well removed from the campus drive when confronting the entry gate, a scaled-down Kyoto prototype. Mature planting sequesters the interior space from activity beyond, and directs the focus inward to a naturalistic pond. The gentle transition from water to land is achieved with a variety of textures and forms. Wispy, bright green rushes, short, shaggy-barked posts, cobbles, and carefully inset boulders camouflage unusually well the edge of the concrete-lined pond. Dark still waters pose an illusory depth, reflecting weeping willows and lending a dramatic flair to the koi, which are all the more bewitching when gold and Mandarin orange appear and disappear into the shadows.

There is a moment in a walk on the curving path to the teahouse when the white-trunked birch trees (an alkaline-tolerant alternative to Japanese maple) and the splash of a small waterfall are a perfect abbreviation for woodland experience. And that, after all, is the intention of the Japanese garden, to take a chapter of nature and reduce it to a few pungent phrases.

Landscape architect Edward R. Lovell traveled to Japan to seek inspiration for this project, visiting the Imperial gardens. Dr. Koichi Kawana of UCLA advised him on matters of authenticity, and specifically against painting the arched bridge red. The two bridges that traverse the pond are handsomely detailed in wood, and the visual exchange from one to the other is an effective device to enlarge a relatively small space.

Long Beach old-timers recognize Earl Miller's name. Partner in an asphalt paving and curb company, a prosperous business in Southern California's boom years, Miller continued his men on payroll during the Depression, despite an absence of work. When his company was bought by Union Oil, Miller used the proceeds philanthropically, notably for Long Beach Children's Hospital. In another public-spirited gesture the Millers donated to the Long Beach Museum of Art funds to construct a Japanese garden. However, as often is the case when assertive works of architecture are being designed, the landscape architecture seemed an afterthought. Support

was withdrawn, and the funds were redirected by Lorraine Miller Collins to this project at Cal State Long Beach as a memorial to her first husband.

The Earl Burns Miller Japanese Garden is too little known, although for many on campus—an enrollment of 32,000 makes Cal State Long Beach the second largest in the state college system—it is a part of student life. This is due mainly to regular operating hours, especially in comparison to sequestered Japanese gardens elsewhere.

DONALD C. TILLMAN
WATER RECLAMATION PLANT
JAPANESE GARDEN

VAN NUYS

With a plush green pile, sod farms carpet the Sepulveda Dam Flood Control Basin. In the distance, tiny figures stoop in the field, and the blue sky looms large. This is the city of Los Angeles, but the emptiness and flat, rural quality recall the Central Valley, California's fertile agricultural corridor. The suggestion of a grand landscape by a lesser one in the Japanese manner sets a fitting metaphorical mood, but it does not begin to prepare you for the startling juxtaposition just down the road: an Imperial Japanese stroll garden alongside a high-tech wastewater treatment plant.

No one says that a treatment plant has to be unattractive, and City Engineer Donald C. Tillman set out to prove this once and for all. Anticipating opposition to a new reclamation facility in the San Fernando Valley from surrounding communities and inspired by a class at UCLA taught by Dr. Koichi Kawana, Tillman proposed a Japanese garden as a site enhancement. The federal grants that underwrite construction of treatment plants, however, are notoriously restrictive when it comes to landscape amenity, so from the Los Angeles Bureau of Sanitation came the funds for the ambitious six-and-a-half-acre garden installation. Since completion in 1983, it has become a vehicle to educate the public about water reclamation. After the escorted garden tour, visitors are introduced to the secondary treatment process, as laden with mystery as Japanese garden symbols.

This is an enormous facility churning out forty million gallons of reusable water per day, part of a larger effort to improve water quality in Santa Monica Bay—and Phase II will double that capacity. The 1984 administration building by Anthony Lumsden is an arresting work of modern architecture, a machinelike expression in concrete and stainless steel. Reclaimed water circulates with a vengeance around its slablike piers, then into the lake that is central to the garden design and mirrors the architectonic visage of the headquarters.

Stroll gardens flourished during the seventeenth to late-nineteenth centuries on the estates of kimono-clad Japanese feudal lords. While some cynics liken control over water in Los Angeles to the rule of an Edo Period fiefdom, the connection at Tillman is strictly one of design heritage. This Japanese garden has the bright and open feeling associated with stroll gardens, the groundcover dichondra suggesting extensive lawns. The plant palette is restrained yet sufficient for seasonal interest: magnolia, cherry, azalea, lotus, and a few Japanese maple, amid black pine and raphiolepis. An evergreen, pink-flowering shrub, raphiolepis is a mainstay in California planter strips, but little used in Japan. At Tillman it appears in profusion shaped in *karikami,* Japanese fashion. The terrain is bermed, and nearly seven hundred boulders, individually placed by five men and a crane, lend a Japanesque, if occasionally spotty, effect. The pools are lined with

Gunite, a type of sprayed concrete, which detracts from the naturalistic effect only when revealed by a low water level.

In a stroll garden, several destinations are linked by a path along which a sequence of compositions unfolds. Here, the focal point may be as simple as a well-pruned bough or as intricate as the waterfall, its three tiers representing heaven, man, and earth. It is in pursuit of these smaller compositions, like a photographer framing a shot, that the Tillman Japanese Garden is best taken in. Viewed across its many inlets and islands, or from above on the observation deck,

sheer size overtakes the poetry of its subtler moments. The esteemed designer Dr. Kawana takes pleasure in arriving at a certain stone lantern, and securing a glimpse from one of the arbors, perhaps the one draped with wisteria. Another designer of Japanese gardens who observed the Tillman was taken by the artful arrangement of three Buddha stones (*sanson*) and by the marshlike planting of iris, which implies a scene in the eleventh-century *Tales of the Ise.*

The promenade begins at a tortoise island. A reference to longevity, it is a large grassy mound surrounded by gravel that also happens to conceal a two-story sewage diversion structure. In this dry garden (*karesansui*), the gravel is not raked, except where it abuts a symbolic shoreline. What a sensible, low-maintenance solution, with centuries of tradition behind it: no lines are needed to simulate waves because it represents a quiet sea. At the far end of the walk, garden features are deliberately more numerous and compactly positioned. A structure in the Shoin style is used for receptions, and holds a traditional four-and-a-half-tatami-mat room. Members of a local tea club bow in humility under the waist-high doorway to the inner sanctum where the ritual tea ceremony is conducted.

You are permitted to experience the Donald C. Tillman Japanese Garden at your own pace at designated times if you have previously attended the docent-led orientation.

DESERT

GARDENS

Moorten Botanical Garden

I had never met anyone like Patricia Moorten, but my husband had. He's fourth-generation Californian and has known similar personalities in his family circle. Pat Moorten is the kind of self-made Westerner with a need to collect, but no particular need to conform, who would brook no obstacles to her interest in botany. She and her long, lean husband Chester, known to all as Cactus Slim, shared a passion for gemstones and desert plant life, and a certainty of intention that fostered a singular botanic garden.

Other gardens with origins in private hands prospered in their time in concert with the considerable fortunes of their proprietors; at the Moorten's, which is still family owned, the garden was not a privilege of wealth but the well-earned product of inquisitive minds and a prospector's outlook. In fact, they were prospectors too, vivacious Pat and Cactus Slim, plying the Rainbow's End Gold Mine near the Joshua trees, in addition to

the business of supplying desert plants and seed. These days, son Clark and the grandchildren help run the garden, and artifacts of the mining operation can be seen on tour.

What exhilarating trips the Moortens must have had in the 1930s, heading out in the heat to wide open country and on down through Mexico to the Guatamala line. They drove a '29 Buick touring car, its body cut off behind the big front seat. Up over the back, with the spontaneous, slapdash inventiveness that characterized Californians, they built a utility box to transport supplies and plants. An early camper of sorts, it had a fifty-gallon gas tank, a fifty-gallon water tank, and a shower that hung off the side of the door. They would go where elephant trees grow: "In Baja California, under the spell of moonlight," Cactus Slim told *National Geographic* in 1957, "I have seen groves whose brown trunks and branches suggested a herd of elephants."

The collections are arranged geographically within the garden in more than a dozen desert regions. In the Baja,

as expected, stands the elephantine *Bursera microphylla,* along with mesquite, ironwood, and organ pipe cactus, this last one of many bristly residents here with pictographic common names, like mink's tail, fish hook, cat's claw, golden barrel, and candelabra.

There follows the upside-down boojum (*Idria columnaris*) and its relative, an unusual white-flowered ocotillo. (Flame-colored blossoms tip the spiny, canelike branches of the local species.) Then into the Mojave: a Spanish bayonet (*Yucca baccatta*), reputedly the tallest known example of its kind, and on to Arizona, with cholla in bloom and prickly pear bearing its dark red, almost black, juice-laden fruit. Next to a living giant saguaro a portion of a saguaro skeleton is displayed. The vascular tubes that support the hefty weight of the impressive, pronged silhouette are but one example of the natural bric-a-brac that accompanies this living collection, from ancient fossils and petrified wood to last year's dove's nest festooned with a remnant of white bridal veil. (Many weddings have taken place in the small, well-used courtyard adjacent to the house, with its whimsical backdrop, "Little Tahquitz Falls," and a swooping palm.)

The garden is very dense; they say more than three thousand varieties are on view on the three-acre site. A mazelike trail penetrates a thicket of furrowed, thorn-bearing forms. Propped at the base of selected species are hand-lettered signs on ashen gray scrap wood for plant

identification. The folkloric quality of the plaques has its charm but belies the complexity of the collection; supplemental signage with sharp, professional graphics would facilitate the self-guided tour and do deserved justice to the botanic collection.

Despite the growth of downtown Palm Springs to her front step, Mrs. Moorten's place still feels part of the desert. It is located along the Indian Trail to Palm Canyon, a natural preserve under reservation control and native habitat of the grass-skirted California fan palm. At the garden's back fence abruptly rise the San Jacinto Mountains, as they do the full length of the Palm Springs commercial core, as stolid a barrier to development as resolute Moorten herself. She recently won a five-year battle to prevent the front portion of her garden from being plowed under for a street-widening project.

The appearance of the mountains changes with the time of day—distinct planes of rock in the morning with pincushion shrubs, a uniform muted purple toward night—but there is always an immediacy to the mountainous terrain that unites the Moorten garden with the Colorado Desert where it began.

Mrs. Moorten glides through the garden as a hostess would. "Are you enjoying the collection?" she inquires of visitors, sometimes to their bewilderment, when tourists do not recognize her as founder and namesake. She is also a lecturer and author; her handbook *Desert Plants for Desert Gardens* is an excellent

guide to design applications. I was delighted to find it at the Strybing Arboretum library in San Francisco, as it has been out of print for some time. A revised edition is in the making.

By the 1950s, Palm Springs had become a Hollywood hangout and the Moortens were part of the scene. Cactus

Slim, character actor and contortionist, was a stand-in to Howard Hughes due to an uncanny resemblance to the eccentric millionaire. The Moortens landscaped the homes of numerous celebrities, and names like Walt Disney, Lily Pons, and Hoagy Carmichael crop up in conversation. There is an arresting black-and-white glossy on an end table in the museumlike living room. A youthful Patricia Moorten is at the Palm Springs Airport in a full-skirted, cactus-appliquéd dress, presenting a ceremonial bouquet to Gov. Ronald Reagan and wife Nancy.

We enter a greenhouse devoted exclusively to cactus—a "cactarium," the word coined by the Moortens—and it is even more densely packed with plants than the grounds outside. Under white painted glass the light is diffuse, setting thorns aglow, the air hot, dry, and comforting. A snakelike cactus from South America slithers the length of the greenhouse and back. There is a contingent of pudgy, furry creatures, *Mammillaria plumosa*, that were discovered in a cluster "on a deep expedition" in lower Mexico, a rare totem pole cactus, a synod of bishop's caps, and on and on. It is an encyclopedia of shape, and Patricia Moorten, in a straw sun hat and bright yellow shirt, smiles with satisfaction. She is in her element.

THE LIVING DESERT

"It's a Chamber of Commerce day," chirped the radio DJ as we tooled along the relentless commercial strip to Palm Desert southwest from Palm Springs. The weather was comfortable—blue skies and sunny, as broadcast—and we were longing for the desert to begin in earnest. The promised boundary always seemed to be just one more shopping center away. Mercifully, we made a wrong turn and, escaping the tide of urbanization that floods the Coachella Valley, bounded upland into the Santa Rosa Mountains. The highway narrowed, the turns acute around steep, rocky promontories. A cultural attraction serving 130,000 people in a ten-month year couldn't be at the end of a road like this, I thought; still, we needed to leave civilization behind, an instinct too easily frustrated in this growing region, and so we drove on.

Just short of the pass, we pulled out at an overlook several thousand feet high, and in one of those transcendent moments that makes travel worthwhile and compensates for filling stations, phone booths, and frustrating road maps, we felt happily borne away by the invigorating freshness of the air, the splendor of the scenery, the freedom found only on mountaintops. The resinous scent of a single pinecone prolonged the memorable detour as we headed back down. The Indians gathered pinyon pinecones before the large edible seed was released to competing birds and wildlife, forcing the scales open instead by the heat of the fire, which also improved the taste of the pine nut. Pinyon pine trees, Southern California's only single-needled pine, are ancient and extremely slow growing, about a half-inch a year, assuming rain. A large one,

thirty feet tall, can be more than a thousand years old. We felt a certain privilege having met this venerable plant with limited range on its own turf.

Not far from there Ruth Watling lives. She is horticulturist at The Living Desert, a nonprofit nature preserve, zoo, and botanical garden. People have long lived on the fringe of the desert, from the grizzled misanthrope baiting parched and feckless tourists with cold drinks and "last gas" to the new breed of sensitive and aware desert dweller, like Watling, moved by its rhythms and aggressive in its defense. She recounted as an endurance contest eighteen months of county meetings on development issues. The residents dropped out but the developers kept coming.

"They rip out thousand-year-old plants, then go to the nursery and buy one-gallon cans," Watling tells me with exasperation. Among the endangered plants are the pinyon pine (*Pinus monophylla*), California juniper (*Juniperus californica*), and manzanita (*Arctostaphylos glauca*), as well as Joshua trees (*Yucca brevifolia*) that she estimates can be five hundred years old per stem. Watling has a personable method of approaching tractor operators on the verge of uprooting important native plants. In a conversational, not confrontational, way she suggests that the plant be donated to The Living Desert, and this alerts the owner to its intrinsic monetary value. Some developers have at least learned to call and see if the preserve is interested in the

latest victims, but they haven't learned to leave significant plants undisturbed.

In 1953, a farsighted group of individuals anticipated the onslaught of construction and set aside an unspoiled twelve-hundred-acre tract of diversified land—wash, hillside, six miles of trails, borrowed scenery—as a desert preserve. Formally opened in 1970, its educational displays occupy about three hundred acres, with plans to expand certain wildlife exhibits. Since inception, Karen Sausman has been executive director and guiding light.

Any large public garden is home to wildlife as well as plants. Birds, butterflies, lizards, toads, and in some places more exotic creatures, like the roadrunners here and at UC Riverside Botanic Gardens, reside among the plant life. At The Living Desert, the integration of plants and animals is taken a step further with displays of introduced animals: sandcat, meerkat, gila monsters, gazelles, and numerous other desert inhabitants from hummingbirds to bighorn sheep. The concept of desert ecology extends to human habitation as well. An Indian exhibit, with a Cahuilla dwelling and their practical and medicinal plant species, illustrates the role of native Americans in the desert biosystem, and introduces an increasingly popular subject, ethnobotany. The herb called Mormon tea (*Ephedra nevadensis*), for example, is a natural source of the active ingredient in sudafed, as the scientific name implies. A

congested Cahuilla would steep the leaves as tea and drink.

Seven different American deserts are represented, including the Mojave, Upper Colorado, Sonoran, Chihuahuan, and Yuman. A desert is studied, then replicated as accurately as possible, using its signature features. Wary of the ill effects of overinterpretation, Watling cautions, "Don't fry the visitor!" and is determined in her designs to assist viewers to see on their own. The Baja Garden, for example, is modelled on the Vizcaino Desert in the central third of the Baja peninsula. Hillocks and tons of rock emulate the general milieu; juvenile boojum and cardone represent their huge counterparts in the wild, like seedlings standing in for veteran oaks. Completing the scene the day we were there was a brightly colored beach umbrella propped between the dunes, sheltering the folding chairs and easels of two Sunday painters.

In contrast to most gardens, which are surrounded by structure, foliage, or landform, The Living Desert merges with the rugged terrain beyond. The great open spaces of the Western landscape are immediate to this garden experience. When you look at the Mojave display, you see a desert within a desert. When you see palo verde petals covering the ground, the apron of yellow pigment is set off by its complement, the purple hue of distant mountainsides. The rigid forms of exhibition cacti and succulents, spaced naturally apart and optically sharpened in

the arid air, look like an isolated sculpture garden under the dome of blue sky. Strong, architectural shadows are cast graphically upon the concrete walks and sandy byways.

Take the locally common teddy bear cholla (*Opuntia bigelovii*). Glowing straw-colored spines and glochids are so closely set on its jointed limbs that from a distance the plant looks cuddly. In reality, the fearsome spines, covered with a translucent papery sheath, are a survival mechanism, shading the stem and allowing evaporated water to condense and drop back down to the root zone. If Madison Avenue were charged with giving cacti their common names, catchy sobriquets would pitch the natural adaptations, like TufStuf, Thick 'N Thorny, or OUCH. If Palm Springs boosters were to advise, the plants would no doubt be named for celebrities, as much else is, here, and you'd be reading about the Bob Hope Cholla.

Not all desert plants adjust to the harsh environment with barbs and a stiff upper lip. At The Living Desert there are delicate trees and shrubs that seem to dissolve in the light. Typical to a desert wash, a relatively moist and ecologically rich subarea, are trees with a loose, ephemeral cascade of foliage. They cope with lack of water by being leafless most of the year; they hold their ground against the force of flash floods by being deeply rooted. One such is desert willow (*Chilopsis linearis*), used ornamentally throughout the preserve. (A local clone

with plum-colored, tubular blossoms is found near the Education Building.) Palo verde trees (*Cercidium floridum*), aptly nicknamed the "out-of-focus tree" by a photographer friend, shade the parking lot. Their bright green branches conduct photosynthesis. And the quintessence of fuzzy desert figures, the smoke tree (*Dalea spinosa*), is lacking in line entirely, a blue-gray gaseous puff.

A major quality of the gardens is the field of sand and rock between plants. Weeds, the scourge of the dirt gardener, are remarkably absent in the empty space that itself becomes a key garden element. Rock work of various sorts is a sympathetic design component in the hardscape. Hulking, burnished boulders dramatize the Discovery Room courtyard, while nearby a handsome dressed stone wall capped by a pruned hedge of gray-green *Leucophyllum frutescens* has a prim, tailored appearance.

There are many other plant-related features at The Living Desert, including numerous display plots, such as a multicolored mallow garden; for homes with

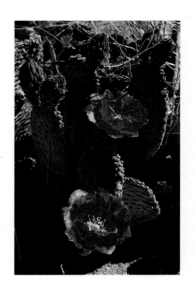

desert-appropriate overhanging eaves, a shade-tolerant demonstration garden; a plant nursery selling species propagated on-site; the surprise of two ponds; a weather station; a bookstore; and more. Respite from the sun being essential for visitors, ramadas—simple, four-posted shade structures—appear repeatedly along the tour.

Understanding the local desert is ultimately what this preserve is about. Follow the Jaeger Nature Trails away from the exhibits and enter the Colorado Desert proper. The Colorado is a low-elevation division of the Sonoran Desert, which reaches up into Arizona and Southern California from Mexico. Normal annual rainfall is three inches, but some years witness twice as much and others practically none. When the temperature measures 120 degrees five feet above the ground, count on 180 degrees at the surface. The reserve is located on the alluvial plain of Deep Canyon, which is the main drainage of the Santa Rosa Mountains. Until a flood-control levee was constructed in 1981, tempestuous floods would roar through here carving channels and depositing silt, rock, and debris. For many people the hike and firsthand evidence of such extreme natural forces will be the most satisfying part of the visit.

BOTANIC

GARDENS

Los Angeles State and County Arboretum

On a trip to Hawaii in 1939, Dr. Samuel Ayres was enchanted by the flowering trees and, like virtually every other tourist before and since, wanted to bring a bit of paradise back home, in particular its paint box of brilliant color. California, it seemed to him, was drabber than need be. In his case, atypically, "home" had a climate hospitable to such notions, and Ayres, a prominent member of the Southern California Horticultural Institute, had the vision, tenacity, and position to make it happen. He traveled to South America, South Africa, the Mediterranean, Australia, and New Zealand collecting and growing plants with which to brighten Southern California. He headed a committee to establish an arboretum where plant material such as he had collected could be grown, and in 1947 a suitable property was purchased by the state from Henry Chandler in the town of Arcadia.

Any place that has "State" in its title had better have scope and substance worthy of the designation, and the Los Angeles State and County Arboretum (LASCA), despite the very limited role played by the state—it is run entirely by Los Angeles County—lives up to the name. It is big, at 127 acres, and it is bountiful. In a scenic, spacious setting, descended from the Rancho Santa Anita, extensive collections proclaim the extraordinary number of plants that are adapted to the mild if dry weather of Southern California.

In all, there are some 30,000 permanent plants on the grounds representing 4,000 species, varieties, or forms. There

are emissaries from temperate regions such as birch, barberry, lilac, and viburnum. In protected locations, there are tender plants from the tropics, such as pseudobombax and plumeria. And there is a bonanza of subtropical material. Major collections include acacia (124 species), bottlebrush (24 species), cycads (175 species), coral trees (27 species), fig trees (79 species), melaleuca (75 species), and thousands of orchids.

Half a million people arrive at LASCA a year, despite the virtual impossibility of reaching the arboretum by public transportation from central Los Angeles. For the casual visitor — tourists, joggers, sweethearts, and Sunday strollers — the appeal of the vast plant

collections is their presentation in dozens of scenarios to experience and explore. There is a jungle garden with primeval cycads; an aquatic garden; idyllic Meadowbrook; an African section; a South American section; an herb garden; a bamboo grove; and on and on. To attain a view of Mount Wilson on a clear day, climb Tallac Knoll, and in the process you will encounter the Pasadena oak. A rare remaining stand of this native tree graces the slope.

Most people start behind the entry pavilion at either the *Sunset Magazine* Demonstration Home Gardens or at the groundcover plots displaying the many alternatives to ordinary lawn in the southland. These exhibits reflect the primacy of education as an arboretum objective, other examples being the Plant Science Library and the Environmental Education Fair that is hosted every spring for elementary school teachers preparing to fulfill that curriculum requirement. Unfortunately, the complementary role of scientific research at the arboretum has declined in recent years.

As you move out by foot or tram, a formal reflecting pool with fountain makes the first impression. It is indicative of the numerous water features that refresh the arboretum but entirely misleading otherwise, because a rambling informality generally prevails. In fact, the first master plan prepared for the arboretum, which was in the formal European tradition typical to estates and early botanic gardens, was rejected by the

board of the California Arboretum Foundation because it was not "up to date." To my thinking, an axial layout framing the San Gabriel Mountains, like that proposed in vain by landscape architect George Kern in 1947, or a more forceful, modern site design would have done more to organize the arboretum and unify its parts.

Presently, a circular road is the central organizing feature for circulation. It circumscribes, yet tends to isolate, the site of three historic buildings adjoining a three-and-half-acre lagoon. Natural lakes are a rare phenomenon in the Los Angeles Basin. This spring-fed sag pond results from seismic activity along the Raymond Hill Fault. The buildings are intrinsic to the saga of this property, and for many visitors a primary destination: the 1839 Hugo Reid adobe, an 1879 coach barn, and E. J. "Lucky" Baldwin's 1885 Queen Anne cottage. The adobe house is surrounded by a prickly pear hedge (*Opuntia tuna*), the landscape barrier typifying the Mission period, which Reid had observed at Mission San Gabriel.

We chose the Australian Section for detailed perusal one day, being in search of the perfect eucalyptus tree to complete a landscape plan. Eucs are often maligned because of the messy habits of one of their kind, the blue gum. But the eucalyptus is an essential part of the California landscape and there are hundreds of species to tantalize designers. As with so many plants, only a limited

number can be found in nurseries. The arboretum grows 150 of the 500 known species, possibly the largest collection outside Australia. We were thrilled by the chance to become acquainted with lesser known examples.

It was sweltering, the kind of day when everything seems to shimmer. In khakis and Panama hats, we were given a lift by car to the outback and, without regard to bearings, plunged right in. We were alone in a dry and camphor-scented realm of gums and yates, moorts, marlocks, mallees, and messmates. With such musical names the Aussies have sorted out this huge genus. The trees are not at all arranged, but are planted in an open and quite disingenuous manner. If there's a logic to the layout, it was not apparent without a guide.

The silence was disturbed by the eucalyptus duff crunching loudly underfoot. We were drawn from one tree to the next by form and size, by leaf color, and by the strikingly different textures of bark, from the smooth, tactile surface on certain gums to the fibrous, twisted armor of the ironbark. The Mindinao gum striped in metallic tones of pink, mauve, apple green, and copper, is painterly in the extreme. Hot, thirsty, and unaccustomedly turned around, we found ourselves as good as lost on the subcontinent, and began to wish that this imaginary trek had been outfitted with some proper gear, specifically canteen and compass.

The pride of the arboretum is the plant introduction program. Since 1958, in the founding spirit of Samuel Ayres, more than a hundred new species or varieties have been presented to the nursery trade, following years of experimentation and trial. For example, the gold medallion tree (*Cassia leptophylla*) and the golden trumpet tree (*Tabebuia chrysotricha*) are showy, small-scale trees nurtured on behalf of the home gardener, the arboretum's target group. Many workhorse plants that we take for granted, like the ubiquitous freeway daisy (*Osteospermum fruticosum*) have their roots, so to speak, at the arboretum.

The introduction program certainly explains a trend or two. It was in about 1979 or 1980 that everywhere at once, up north in Berkeley, appeared an unfamiliar evergreen shrub with eye-catching lavender-blue flowers, in front of fashionable restaurants, alongside brown-shingle houses, in the yards of hilltop homes. Sure enough, in the Australian section at the arboretum was the original blue hibiscus (*Alyogyne huegelii*), introduced to the trade in 1968.

When it comes to public delight, "the animal world has it over the plant world hand over fist," James Folsom, curator of the Huntington Botanical Gardens, had told me, and this is painfully evident at the Los Angeles State and County Arboretum where the trees and shrubs are routinely upstaged by the peacocks. Descendants of three pair of peafowl brought from India by Lucky Baldwin near the turn of the century, they are allowed to roam free, despite a tendency to destroy plant life. Unabashedly they prance, they preen, fanning their train feathers and issuing their piercing cry. Onlookers are thoroughly engaged, while hundreds of superior but overlooked plants recede mutely in the background.

"If only I could teach the peacocks to talk," quipped LuAnn Munns, director of public relations. "At least they could tell people the names of the plants."

UC Irvine Arboretum

Someone should alert Hollywood. Botany is high adventure. After all, the thrill and treachery of other scientific field work has been glorified on screen—Sigourney Weaver as zoologist in the mist, Harrison Ford, archaeologist with a fist. But stardom hasn't arrived for the intrepid botanist who treks remote, inhospitable lands in search of exotic living treasure.

In late February or early March, enter the lower screenhouse at the University of California Irvine Arboretum to see a king's trove of bulbs in synchronous bloom. This is the accumulated wealth of unsung collecting trips to the hinterlands of southern Africa. The flower colors are so saturated, so intense, that they lend unnatural force to such fragile forms. A commanding delicacy is what they possess, a seeming contradiction undeniably expressed in physical form.

The extraordinary plants grow in mundane one-gallon containers set on the ground. You wade slowly down the aisles stooping to admire this ixia, a six-petalled porcelain cup with a dram of chartreuse, or that moraea whose tripartite petals are as iridescent as a peacock feather. The simple screen structure encloses you in an airy vault, but of practical importance, it keeps the bees at bay. Pollinization must be conducted by hand to ensure genetic purity. Rigorous propagation is as essential to the collection as collecting itself.

When Charles J. O'Neill collects for the UCI Arboretum he does not discover vibrant fields of magenta and gold to the crescendo of an imaginary soundtrack, as you might expect. In fact, he barely sees a flower. For the cache he is after is the subtlest treasure of all. Seed. And as any child who has blown a dandelion can tell you, the seeds are produced when the flower is gone. Trips are timed to maximize seed collection of particular varieties, with general locations selected in advance based on the literature and advice of private collectors. "Of course," says O'Neill, "you are looking for a spot five-hundred square feet in an area the size of that." He points from the shoulder with an encompassing sweep of the arm to a long range of hills.

It took two transatlantic trips to attain an elusive moraea in Africa's Sederberg range. On the second, the forest ranger directed tersely, "Look up on that mountain." O'Neill has a pretty good rooting instinct by now, so only six steamy hours later, after a steep ascent in humid, ninety degree heat, with the prospect of nightfall and an arduous return ahead, O'Neill snared his prey. But he didn't pause for exclamations, not a single "Eureka!" Efficiently he deposited the seed in a paper coin envelope, wrote a short identifying label in pencil, and hustled back down. The ranger had indeed told him one more thing. The purlieu of the seductive moraea was also home to a pair of leopards.

"Then there was the time in the Natal province near Kwazulu. The wind was howling, blowing the rain sideways. The clouds were so thick to the ground I couldn't make out cliffs with a five-hundred foot drop-off that were practically in front of me. I tried to find a ravine..." Hollywood, do you read me?

California is one of five Mediterranean-type climates in the world, and the UCI Arboretum has chosen to focus on the flora of one of the other four, southern Africa, an area singularly rich in monocots. Thus the word arboretum is something of a misnomer here. Despite the presence of jacaranda, thorny giraffe acacia (*Acacia*

erioloba), an excellent aloe collection, and numerous other trees and shrubs pleasingly displayed in habitat beds amid grassy paths, the emphasis and pride are the bulbs, corms, and tubers. Theirs is the largest institutional collection (from southern Africa) in the world. It includes primitive species from families otherwise much changed by commercial propagation, such as iris, amaryllis, and lily. Bulbs range from one-quarter the size of the nail on your little finger to larger than a man's closed hand. By limiting the collection to Mediterranean-climate bulbs, the arboretum can dispense with elaborate greenhouses and costly heating systems, as the plants are adapted to natural temperatures here.

The primacy of scientific endeavor at Irvine is complete. Every plant is grown from seeds, even palm. The arboretum maintains a cryogenic gene bank for rare or horticulturally important plant species, which can be held indefinitely, until research calls. Every plant in the living collection is computer-listed in a data bank format adapted from Kew Gardens' international standard. All eight thousand files are complete and in accordance with the most up-to-date taxonomic system. The pelargonium 'Irvine' has become a popular ornamental locally but began as a breeding experiment. In the greenhouse, the flowers are the saleable hues of a cosmetic company, but the objective is more than skin deep. Irvine is conducting research for the USDA, including an effort to breed an

ornithogalum with the tall stem of the white species and the dark orange color of a short-stemmed one (*Ornithogalum dubium*). When finally selected out, the winner will be tissue-cultured by the hundreds of thousands.

Conservation issues loom large at Irvine. It is fundamental that seed and not rootstock be gathered in the field. Wild populations are documented. Endangered species—at present about two hundred of them—are perpetuated by a method of genetically stable propagation that avoids "in-breeding depression." In 1989, the UCI Arboretum hosted an International Bulb Symposium and drew two hundred botanists to discuss matters of taxonomy, floriculture, hybridization, conservation, and ecology, and to strengthen a global network.

Indigenous bulb populations are threatened on many fronts. In Turkey, peasants burrow entire fields of native bulbs for sale to Dutch merchandisers—for propagation, you would hope, but no. The bulbs are put directly on the commercial market, and the native, often rare, rootstock disappears without replenishment. There is a move to brand bulbs that have been officially propagated, so that the consumer need not unwittingly participate in the destruction.

Human population growth in certain African tribes has placed unprecedented demand on the bulbs, corms, and tubers used in herbal cures and rituals, again without replanting. O'Neill witnessed this disrupted cycle when he dickered

with a Zulu medicine man for a particular harvested bulb already gone from its native habitat.

A new collection of native California bulbs is burgeoning at the UCI Arboretum in response to the wanton depletion of native bulbs in Northern California by feral pigs, who consume what they forage at the phenomenal rate of several hundred pounds a day. The collection includes *Lilium*, *Brodiaea* and *Calochortus* that, devotees assure me, outdistance even South African varieties for beauty.

A final nod to conservation is a prohibition at this arboretum against teak benches. Their popularization in public gardens and upscale mail-order catalogues contributes to the destruction of tropical rain forests.

The UCI Arboretum is beautifully sited on a gentle slope overlooking the San Joaquin Marsh wildlife preserve, part of the University of California wetlands system, and the aforementioned hills beyond. It is an unusually expansive view in this dense megalopolis, and absent from the vista are freeway and subdivision. However, the twelve-acre site that was barley fields not so long ago has become valuable Orange County real estate, and it seems only a matter of time until the ultimate conservation campaign will need to be mounted to preserve the site of the arboretum itself.

FULLERTON ARBORETUM

Only at the Fullerton Arboretum would you find a spunky sapling four feet high sporting this forward-looking sign: "New Caledonia pine. A towering columnar tree up to 200 feet tall." For the Fullerton has its youth, and the fullness of youth's promise. Grand estates and long-established collections may impress us with their bounty or astound us with the immensity of mature trees, but the framework has been set and ambitions achieved. At Fullerton, in contrast, the arboretum as a whole seems as dynamic as a growing plant.

This is not to suggest that there is little to see here, for the pleasure of the place is real, the collections satisfying, a testimonial to what can be accomplished in ten years in the warm California sun. Take the entry, a welcoming seasonal display of forthright amaryllis, red-flowered kangaroo paw (*Anigozanthus flavidus*), golden daisy bush (*Gamolepis chrysanthemoides*), and a drought-tolerant slope awash with the pink translucent glow of Mexican evening primrose (*Oenothera berlandieri*). Add water features and winding paths, and Fullerton's founding objective is accomplished with aplomb: to provide an alternative environment amid the rapid and intense urbanization of Orange County. For many Orange County children, a visit to the Fullerton Arboretum is their first experience of the great outdoors.

A Sierra Nevada–inspired waterfall adds sparkle and lively sound to the entry display. On the practical side, it initiates the recirculating system of streams and ponds that helps to structure the garden design and readily attracts songbirds, waterfowl, and other wildlife. Because water features do not need time to mature, their use is an excellent strategy

to give the arboretum an impression of completion and permanence.

Following the stream you will find the only carnivorous plant bog constructed in Southern California, the Temperate Zone collection, and the Tropical Zone with its enormous ombu tree, seventy feet tall and six feet in girth. Propagated from the patriarchal ombu at the Huntington Botanical Gardens, this upstart was planted from a five-gallon can just ten years ago. Compare that to the slow rate of tree growth in our country's colder climes, where ten short summers would nudge a seedling oak just four feet closer to the sky. While the comparison is somewhat unfair—the ombu (*Phytolacca dioica*) is fleshy, like an herb; the oak is woody, as are most trees we are familiar with—the fact remains that thanks to climate, trees and plants have inaugurated a sense of place on these twenty-six acres that belies a decade's time. (Numerous other exhibits include palms, moist and dry; plants of the Canary Islands; a beehive; and a historical orchard of fruit trees economically important to early Orange County agriculture.)

But there is more than climate to credit with this institution's precocious success. A town-and-gown effort has produced a hybrid facility that draws from community life and campus life equally. The arboretum operates under a joint-powers agreement between the trustees of the California State University and the Redevelopment Agency of the City of

Fullerton. The arboretum enjoys a broad base of support: hundreds turn out for pruning demonstrations, members cultivate vegetable plots, the California Rare Fruit Growers maintains an orchard, and college students pursue course work.

In addition to the arboretum's support of the Cal State curriculum, there is an emphasis here on elementary school education. The plant collection is chosen not for rarities but to illustrate concepts basic to ecology and botany. One segment of the garden, for example, is devoted to deciduous trees. The children of winter warmth and summer smog must be taught that some trees lose their leaves in response to short days and cool nights, then leaf out again in spring. Furthermore, they are instructed, the leaves of certain of those incredibe deciduous trees turn beautiful colors before dropping in the fall. For all the subtropical species in Southern California, none brought home to me as strongly the blessedness of the climate as this section at the Fullerton Arboretum. Imagine a land where the skeletal beauty of winter branches or, to others, the dreariness of long, gray days is not second nature, but must be learned on a field trip.

A more sophisticated concept, convergent evolution, is illustrated in the Arid Zone of the Fullerton Arboretum. Convergent evolution is the tendency of plant species in different geographic regions and with dissimilar genetic backgrounds to evolve the same strategies for coping with similar environmental circumstances. In the Mediterranean climates of California, Turkey, and Chile, three chaparral species have evolved mahogany-colored bark and stiff, medium-sized evergreen leaves with toothed edges. The toyon (*Heteromeles arbutifolia*), the strawberry tree (*Arbutus unedo*), and the Chilean *Kageneckia oblonga*, collected by Fullerton staff in the matorral, cope with the wet-winter/dry-summer cycle in the same adaptive fashion.

At the center of the grounds is a Queen Anne cottage, the 1894 office and residence of a Fullerton physician. Saved from demolition and relocated to this property in 1972, it acts as a center of gravity as any home in a garden would. Back at the garden's entry, the administration offices and a horticulture

library, open to the public, are sheltered in two trailers that were used for the Team Handball venue at the 1984 Los Angeles Olympics. An angled trellis and elevated deck, well-detailed and decorated with flowering plants, unite the portables with an easy indoor-outdoor connection in the California landscape tradition. Like the arboretum itself, these workaday structures look surprisingly grounded, although they will eventually be replaced by a permanent administration and education building.

THE MILDRED E. MATHIAS BOTANICAL GARDEN, UCLA

WESTWOOD

The Mildred E. Mathias Botanical Garden is more readily accessible to more people than any other major public garden from Santa Barbara south. Open without fee seven full days a week, it is within walking distance — a convenience unheard of in Southern California — for the fifty-thousand students, faculty, and staff at UCLA, where it occupies eight acres at the southeast corner of campus. Ironically, though, this botanic garden suffices with a small budget, a part-time director with many other responsibilities, and without the "Friends of" support group for development and outreach programs that reinforces other public gardens, even other university facilities.

The garden seems never to have overcome having been remaindered from an original thirty-one acres, and there is an unspoken vulnerability to campus growth that persists due to its location alongside hospital, medical, and dental schools, which, as a rule, hunger to expand. Other public gardens in removed or exclusive locations — many with restricted visiting hours — are tended to a fare-thee-well and demand a premeditated excursion. The Mildred E. Mathias Botanical Garden invites a casual stroll on an ordinary day, and has assumed a relaxed, almost untamed character.

The Mildred E. Mathias Botanical Garden is situated along the only natural remnant of a ravine (now mostly filled and built upon) that once carved a course halfway up campus to Dickson Court. Wandering the botanic garden at the rim of the slope, where the bird song begins, you are eye to eye with the tops of trees rooted in the hollow below, an Alice in Wonderland sensation. The fronds of California fan palms (*Washingtonia filifera*) — charter members of the collection of twenty-five palm species representing every tropical region — are close enough to detect tip damage, evidence of a developing fungus that could disfigure

the stand. Decomposed-granite paths edged informally with mondo grass and liriope follow hillside contours down through the dark wooded glen to a voluble creek with aquatic plants, a cool and covert spot for dalliance or midday assignation.

Other than greenhouse and lath house, the garden is free of structures, but it could hardly be called "open space," it is so densely planted. According to the brochure, there are 4000 species in 275 families, and many of these are full-grown trees, the garden dating from 1930. Recent efforts to open up the canopy—to make room for new collections and to abrogate shade—have meant tree removal and the inevitable hue and cry that accompany even well justified use of the axe. Tree removal has permitted establishment of a lily bed to demonstrate variation in form within a single plant family; a small section of Hawaiian native plants; an airy knoll for sun-loving Mediterranean plants; and several groupings of plants from montane tropical forests, including a pocket of the showy Vireya rhododendrons from Malaysia, which bloom in late September.

Rearing their heads like the fan palms, the dawn redwoods (*Metasequoia glyptostroboides*) are an intriguing part of the gymnosperm collection. Gymnosperms (plants with exposed seeds) include conifers, maidenhair tree, podocarpus, and araucaria, and were long ago a much more dominant component of the earth's vegetation—hence their frequent appearance in prehistoric dioramas. Prior to 1941, the dawn redwood was known only from fossils found in North America, Europe, and Asia. Imagine the commotion in the botany world that year surrounding the discovery of living specimens of this tree in eastern Szechuan on the Yangtse River, where it is called "water larch" by the Chinese.

The dawn redwoods at the Mildred E. Mathias Botanical Garden, grown from seed collected in China in 1947, are unusually tall—reputedly the tallest of their kind in the United States—and resemble slender coast redwoods competing for light in a forest. The novelty of the dawn redwood has not worn off; this deciduous conifer is invariably hailed and welcomed back from prehistory wherever its pyramidal form is spied in the cultivated landscape. Barren in winter, it is graced in spring with nature's most resilient, fresh green foliage, and could just as easily have been named "pliant sequoia."

Among the Australian species here, the most outstanding—quite literally—are the sky-high rose gums (*Eucalyptus grandis*), which soar a neck-craning two

hundred feet tall. There is a fine specimen of myrtle willow (*Agonis flexuosa*), which was given sufficient room to spread its branches of blue-green, peppermint-scented foliage. Beside the path, a Mindinao gum (*Eucalyptus deglupta*), surprisingly from the Philippines, since we expect gums to be from Australia, reflects the late afternoon sun, its multicolored bark shining against the deepening dusk of the canyon below. "My ideal," confided John Hall in the western light, "is an adobe house with unmown grass and a grove of Mindinao gum."

Hall is manager of this botanic garden and runs maintenance operations from a small dusty shed resembling a field station for its shelves of faded books, an upright manual typewriter, and the flapping screen door. Green electric carts (their twenty-four-volt system recharged every night) ply the narrow garden paths on daily rounds. Maintenance is hampered by heavy soils, oak root fungus, root competition, and the adventive weed called African grass.

For a literary view of affairs, consult the *Ancient Poets Guide to UCLA Gardens* by Helen Caldwell, a tour of the botanic ravine via Greek and Roman verse. It is a charming reminder as well that the Latin or scientific name for many plants is the same as the common name known to the Romans over two thousand years ago. Another informative booklet, *The University Garden,* is a guide to landscape planting at UCLA that demonstrates the admirable commitment to horticulture on

this campus. Both are published by the botanical garden.

In 1979, for distinguished contributions to horticulture and dedication to the University of California, Dr. Mildred E. Mathias was recognized with the naming of the botanic garden in her honor. Its director from 1956 to 1974, she has been retired for fifteen years but nonetheless comes to the department every day to teach or study, save for periods of collecting while leading UC Extension travel courses. Dr. Mathias has botanized in remote locations from Africa to Southeast Asia, although her name is most closely associated with the flora of Costa Rica. She was admiringly described to me as the kind of highly accomplished person who is easy to talk with and makes others feel comfortable. With that in mind I called her on the phone to inquire about the rumored demise of holistic botany.

The rise to prominence of molecular botany has siphoned scientific funding from the study of whole organisms, the pursuit for which botanic gardens are made. Are the gardens suffering as a result? "On the contrary," Dr. Mathias responded. "Botanic gardens are earning increasing recognition and support for their role in the conservation of rare species as the tropical rain forests disappear." As for the alleged competition between botanical factions, Dr. Mathias views the forking of routes as an advancement. "It only shows," she said, "there is still a lot to learn."

QUAIL BOTANICAL GARDENS

Rancho de las Flores was the auspicious name for a modest board and batten ranch house on twenty-five acres that became the nucleus of Quail Botanical Gardens. Of its owner Ruth Baird Larabee, who donated the estate to San Diego County in 1957, little is known, not even her appearance. She died in a hotel fire in London, and no photographs of her remain. The cork oaks are her survivors, their powerful multitrunked figures forming one of largest groves in the country. With the thrift of a countrywoman, she had salvaged nursery discards to augment collections from her travels, little by little surrounding the house with myriad plants.

Shaping the donation into a botanic garden has fallen to the Quail Botanical Gardens Foundation and curator Gilbert Voss. Voss has gradually rearranged and supplemented the material, bringing system and order. The Chilean *Puya alpestris*, for example, descended from Larabee's garden, is now displayed with other bromeliads and plants of like geographic origin. Voss steers the garden in a scientific direction, yet remains available to the public for more prosaic concerns. I watched him fielding questions from home gardeners in the breezeway of the visitor center, a structure made surprisingly tropical in this semiarid landscape by an overhanging jacaranda tree, Zulu fig (*Ficus nekbudu*), and the pendulous white trumpets of *Brugmansia aurea*.

Indeed, at the Quail Botanical Gardens a tropical complexion overlays a rural disposition. In the rolling hills of Encinitas north of San Diego where the

subdivisions thin out, alstroemeria, carnations, and poinsettias are produced for the flower trade. At Quail, jubilant hibiscus is a signature flower, and, early on, this was the first public garden to display the superb but difficult proteas. An orchard of subtropical fruit includes guava, macadamia nut, and sapote; palm fronds shelter the nursery stand; and a waterfall ensconced in palms, bananas, and tree ferns is suggestive of Maui and the snaking road to Hana. Throughout the garden, a wild variety of leaf shapes and sizes heightens the equatorial mood.

The Quail Botanical Gardens is not laid out for purely decorative effect, nor is it a replicated jungle. It is the kind of botanical garden that repeatedly halts your walk along rambling dirt paths for a second look at the unfamiliar. Burly-legged dragon trees (*Dracaena draco*) with their tufted sprays of branches. The metallic silver tree (*Leucadendron argenteum*). Bright yellow bells (*Tecoma stans*), a flowering shrub that can be trained as a showy tree in only the mildest climates, as it is here. Especially striking is a grove of Himalayan fishtail palms (*Caryota urens*) at the foot of Palm Canyon, their papery trunks so white that even in the shade they seem illuminated.

Another signature plant and symbol of the exotic is bamboo. The linear strength and rhythmic pattern of its rigid stems are not lost on illustrators, and a poster prominently featured in the bookshop entices you to seek the bamboo section. An irregular planting in what

resembles an abandoned field, the display neglects the design potential of this architectural plant form, but redeems itself botanically. Quail is said to possess the most diverse collection of bamboo in the world, and here are found its south Asian species. They range in form from tall slender poles (*Bambusa tuldoides*) to hefty arched stalks with the girth of a firehose (*B. beecheyana*), and in color from dense, dark green foliage (*B. malingensis*) to brilliant stalks of citron green and orange-ochre (*Phyllostachys vivax*). Surprisingly, the largest genus of bamboo (140 species) is found in the Americas, being dispersed from northern Mexico to the tip of South America. Feathery *Chusquea coronalis* is an example of it, one of numerous New World bamboos grown throughout the gardens. (The only species native to the United States, *Arundinaria gigantea,* from the South, is being established for eventual display.)

Behind the scenes, the Quail Botanical Gardens operates a bamboo quarantine greenhouse because imported bamboo plants, being grasses, must be kept in strict isolation for one year. (The State of California is checking for nematodes; the federal government, tropical rusts.) It is the largest facility of its kind in the United States.

A pleasant enclosed garden adjoins the former residence. Defined by a masonry block wall, it has a tidy geometry quite unlike the rest of the gardens. A colorful ceramic wall fountain with spout in the guise of a mustachioed face is also atypical at Quail, which does not traffic in garden ornament. Enter through wood gates, painted red, to a tended lawn surrounded by ferns and fall-blooming begonias. Under twisted spikes of Hollywood juniper grow holly fern (*Cyrtomium falcatum*), birds' nest fern (*Asplenium nidus*), and the ebony-trunked black tree fern of New Zealand (*Cyathea medullaris*), among other species. This agreeable spot was inaugurated by one of the many plant societies affiliated with Quail.

After crossing the asphalt parking lot, oddly deprived of shade trees, our attention is shifted back to San Diego County. On an additional four acres of parkland, the focus is the chaparral plant community of local hillsides. Pamphlets for a self-guided tour, posted where the native trail begins, describe how the Kumeyaay Indians utilized these plant resources. For a current perspective on ethnobotany, Voss, who is co-authoring a book on the plant life of the Huichol Indians, recommends Gary Nabhan's *Enduring Seeds*.

CALIFORNIA

NATIVE

PLANT

GARDENS

RANCHO SANTA ANA BOTANIC GARDEN

CLAREMONT

A look at the table of contents of the scholarly journal *Aliso* published by the Rancho Santa Ana Botanic Garden plainly illustrates the difference between a gardener's view of plants and a scientist's. The RSABG is dedicated to the study, cultivation, and preservation of California native plants. It is a preeminent scientific institution, with an eighty-five-acre living collection of California plant communities, a sophisticated technical laboratory, a library of forty thousand volumes and an herbarium of over one million species. In affiliation with the Claremont Colleges, it offers post-graduate degrees in botany.

Rancho Santa Ana Botanic Garden is widely recognized for the native plant cultivars it has introduced to the nursery trade, and signature species form the backbone of the display in Claremont. Drought-tolerant workhorses like baccharis 'Twin Peaks,' ceanothus 'Ray Hartman,' manzanita 'Point Reyes,' and mahonia 'Golden Abundance' are among

dozens of now-commonplace varieties originating here that have changed the nature of landscape gardening in California.

If you like art museums that feature a single school of painting — say, the Impressionists at the lamented Jeu de Paume in Paris — you will respond favorably to this collection of plants. You will intuitively decipher among varieties of a single species marked similarities that attest to kinship and intriguing differences that are the essence of character. Gradations of green, variation in flower color or size, particulars of growth habit and leaf shape — these are the subtleties that reward the observant.

If indeed you are partial to Impressionism, you will thrill to the Rancho Santa Ana Botanic Garden at its peak in spring. In late March, the profuse and simultaneous bloom of California lilac (deep and periwinkle blue) and fremontia (saturated golden yellow) evokes the liberated brushwork of the French masters and their plein-air descendants in

217

Southern California, such as William Wendt. In intense California light, these massed native shrubs become ten- to fifteen-foot-tall murals of color. Although conceived for purposes of botanical study, the heady combination of blue and yellow adheres to Gertrude Jekyll's esthetic wisdom in *Colour Schemes for the Flower Garden*: "Any experienced colourist knows that the blues will be more telling—more purely blue—by the juxtaposition of rightly placed complementary color."

A private institution, the RSABG is the legacy of Suzanna Bixby Bryant. Weary of a socialite's existence, she applied herself to the management of the Bixby family ranch in Orange County and, by extension, to tree planting there. In 1926, she conceived of a botanic garden as a memorial to her father John W. Bixby, a courageous pioneer and outdoorsman who came to California at age twenty-five and died before turning forty. In the hills bordering the Santa Ana River Valley, Suzanna Bixby Bryant set aside for the purpose 160 acres of family property, ranging in elevation from 450 to 1100 feet and possessed of exhilarating views.

According to *A Short History of the Rancho Santa Ana Botanic Garden* by former director Philip A. Munz, she called in for advice none other than Charles Sprague Sargent of the Arnold Arboretum at Harvard University. (The relationship continues today, as RSABG works closely with the Center for Plant

Conservation located at the Arnold.) Sargent would have been eighty-five at that time, still active by most standards, but in comparison to the vigor of his remarkable career, enfeebled, and within a year of his death. He urged the drafting of a working plan for the botanic garden and suggested that Ernest Braunton of Los Angeles, garden columnist and expert, undertake the assignment.

Dr. W. L. Jepson provided Braunton a comprehensive list of native plants. Jepson heads an impressive roster of names synonymous with California botany who came to serve the RSABG, including Theodore Payne and former director Lee Lenz. As a consequence, many definitive publications have emanated from RSABG, such as *A California Flora and Supplement* by Munz and Keck and *California Native Trees and Shrubs* by Lenz and Dourley.

Judging by old photographs, the original Rancho Santa Ana site was quite extraordinary. An adobe administration building in the Spanish style presided regally over the historic grounds, and there Suzanna Bixby Bryant performed as managing director of the botanic garden until her sudden death in 1946.

In 1951, the RSABG was moved in five-gallon cans and by the planting of seeds to a mesa in the San Gabriel foothills familiar to Mrs. Bryant, who had graduated from nearby Scripps College. In the new location, research and education in native California plants have achieved international recognition for the institution. After the move, much of the original garden was destroyed in a fire; more recently, the Orange County property was sold to developers.

Today, under Director Thomas Elias, RSABG is again undergoing a master-plan process. An ambitious rearrangement of the garden designed by the landscape architectural firm Environmental Planning and Design of Pittsburgh offers the RSABG two new beginnings: a relocated main entrance off Indian Hill Boulevard (leading to a logical loop road), and a renewed commitment to public education about native plants and conservation. The first step is the development of the California

cultivars garden, placing RSABG's achievements firmly in the center of the grounds. Hybrid iris, coral bells, and monkey flower, along with ceanothus, manzanita, fremontia, and others, will grace a prominent area presently used for unsightly experimental plots.

The plan takes advantage at last of the commanding presence of Mount Baldy. Over ten thousand feet high, it will unflinchingly terminate the principal axis of the reconfigured plan. In the foreground will be a meadow of wildflowers, a pertinent and effective use of the mesa landform, reminiscent of the *parti* at the Santa Barbara Botanic Garden. This striking postcard image of blossom-strewn field and snow-capped peak will become a trademark that makes the botanic garden more memorable and more marketable to the general public.

Meanwhile, collecting goes on. Garden scientists led by Dr. Elias travel to China and the USSR to collect specimens and seed plasm, and in San Luis Obispo County, the southernmost outcrop of serpentine in the state, staffers are discovering rare and unusual plants on the ranch of Ernest A. Bryant III, chairman of the RSABG board and Suzanna Bixby Bryant's grandson.

SANTA BARBARA BOTANIC GARDEN

SANTA BARBARA

Wandering the Santa Barbara Botanic Garden feels like a gentle hike through serendipitously adjoining plant communities. The displays are naturalistic and blend into their setting, an exceptional site up Mission Canyon where the handsome tile-roofed town begins to give way to Los Padres National Forest. Many fine coast live oaks punctuate the garden, and enormous sandstone boulders deposited by glaciation stand sentinel along the trails.

Honey-colored stone is Santa Barbara's characteristic but unsung landscape element. Countywide, the local rock lends its pleasing hue and texture to retaining walls, garden structures, and planting designs. Here, Cathedral Peak and La Cumbre Peak form a sandstone skyline, a theatrical backdrop to the Botanic Garden's stage. There is an immediacy to the Santa Ynez mountain range. In spring, its skirt of chaparral dispenses a resinous, Mediterranean

scent to the garden below, and in winter, the white flush of big-pod ceanothus (*Ceanothus megacarpus*) in bloom extends the Botanic Garden's show of flowering native plants.

The Santa Barbara Botanic Garden welcomes exploration at will, an invitation made all the sweeter because despite the noble history of garden making in Santa Barbara, opportunity to partake of it is limited. The sequestered estates of Montecito, some of the finest in the state, withhold their grandeur, the arboretum of noted plantsman Francesco Franceschi is open but sadly dishevelled, and the garden cloister at Mission Santa Barbara, extolled in its time for floral abundance, is cordoned off.

The Botanic Garden collections are arrayed on hillside, plateau, and canyon wall by plant type or by habitat—manzanita and ceanothus sections, arroyo, desert, woodland, and island sections. But the calling card is its central meadow, a field of wildflowers as foreground to the peaks: blue-eyed grass,

farewell-to-spring, lupine, foothill pen-
stemon, and of course, California poppy,
with an orange so intense that early
sailors navigated by a patch of it on Point
Conception, due west of here. The colors
of spring and summer yield to the golden
arch of goldenrod and red California
fuchsia in fall.

The simple scheme of the wildflower
meadow has been amplified with informative displays. Low-maintenance perennial
bunch grasses were introduced in 1981,
responding to the demise of native grass-
lands in many areas of the state from
livestock grazing, agriculture, and urbanization, and foretelling popular interest
in grasses for ornamental landscaping. A
recent addition to the meadow's edge is a
decorative border of native plants: ver-
bena, yarrow, fragrant salvias, sticky
monkey flower, a low-growing fremontia,
and others. Interpretive signage that
explains this drought-tolerant alternative
to the English perennial border is one
example of a lively program for public
awareness commencing at the Botanic
Garden. Preparation of a new master
plan is also underway.

There are about 5100 native plant
species in California. Of these, about a
third are endemic; that is, they occur here
and nowhere else. The flora of the state is
extremely varied due to a diversity of
settings—desert, alpine, coastal, interior
valley. However, not all native species are
ornamental, and many that are of horticultural interest are not suited to the
maritime climate of Santa Barbara. It is

too humid for some desert species, and too mild for certain alpine material that must undergo a period of winter cold. The quaking aspen (*P. tremuloides*) of montane meadows, for example, does not cope well near sea level. Brought here in a five-gallon can, it fared adequately the first year, declined in the second, and never made it past the third. The black cottonwood (*Populus trichocarpa*) of mountain streams, on the other hand, performs well. Such constraints remind us to appreciate that the culture of over nine hundred native California species at the Santa Barbara Botanic Garden is not without trial and error.

Nor is plant breeding a simple matter, as new materials are developed for the nursery trade. Only the patient need apply: a multistep process from pollinization to field test takes at least two years, and then, even with the good fortune of a first-rate plant, the mites might fancy it too. The California rose (*Rosa californica*) is one of many native species advanced by Dara Emery, plantsman at the Santa Barbara Botanic Garden for thirty years. He is seeking a drought-tolerant, low-maintenance rose by crossing the pink single-flowered native with miniature roses and hardy *Rosa rugosa*. When I admired one offspring with rose hips like cinnamon red hots, Emery

pointed out that certain plants make good parents because they transmit desirable genes, even if they don't exhibit the sought-after trait themselves.

In 1926, from an automobile parked beneath the meadow oaks, Dr. Elmer J. Bissell and his wife Ervanna Bowin Bissell set out and tended the first plants of the Blaksley Botanic Garden. Sponsored by philanthropist Anna Blaksley Bliss, the garden's purpose was to research and display the plant communities of the Pacific Slope. Ten years later, the garden's purpose narrowed to California natives, and in 1939, the name was changed to Santa Barbara Botanic Garden. It remains an independent, nonprofit institution.

In recent years, beneath the oaks, a festive community event called "Give the Earth a Hand" has convened in September. It exemplifies the educational thrust of Santa Barbara Botanic Garden and the increasing importance of all botanic gardens for environmental action. "Ecology comes first," explained Garden Director Dr. David Young. "The habitat must be preserved. Second best is to preserve the species. That is the responsibility of botanic gardens in the twenty-first century." It is estimated that thirty-four species of native California plants are extinct already, and fifteen hundred are endangered. "At no time since the end of the Cretaceous period, sixty-five million years ago, has there been such a rapid rate of species extinction of the world's most vital resource, plants .... Although the garden's physical resources are limited to sixty-five acres, the value of what we can do with our physical resources for science and humanity has no limits."

A scientific focus of the Santa Barbara Botanic Garden is the isolated, and in cases endangered, plant life of the Channel Islands. Santa Barbara's off-

shore islands appear and disappear with the tide of coastal fog, and like Bali Hai, beckon with a come-hither mystique. Biologists are justifiably lured. The eight Channel Islands are compared to the Galapagos archipelago for the uniqueness and abundance of life found there. The Botanic Garden has conducted numerous research and conservation projects on island topics, mounted 25,000 sheets of island flora (in a 90,000-sheet herbarium), and installed a living collection. On a clear day, begin your visit to the bush poppy, buckwheat, and tree mallow in the island section with a diversion to the east ridge of the Botanic Garden (across Mission Canyon Road), and gaze across the Santa Barbara Channel at the northernmost islands.

The island ironwood (*Lyonothamnus floribundus*) is a rare and remarkable tree that vanished from the mainland six million years ago, but which persists in two distinct forms on the islands. At the Botanic Garden, the more picturesque Santa Cruz Island ironwood, with its finely serrated leaf margins, can be compared side by side with the Catalina ironwood. Wanting to know more about the appearance of these trees in the wild, I sought staff botanist Steve Junak. He spends about a week every month across the channel, a regimen that explains his mien of tanned fitness, unexpected in the windowless concrete of the herbarium where I found him at work. He described the ironwood's niche: emerging in discreet stands from island chaparral, iron-wood trees show a preference for volcanic soil and northfacing slopes, and among the trunks of peeling red bark the atmosphere is not unlike that in a redwood grove.

Along the creek in the cool canyon above Mission Dam, redwood trees were planted around 1930. They tower now, responding to favorable conditions and supplements of water and acid plant food. In the company of sorrel, yerba buena, sword fern, and ginger, the redwoods look remarkably at home, belying the difficulty of growing these Northern California stalwarts in the southland.

Mission Dam was erected by Chumash Indians in service to the Franciscan order, its wall of sandstone and ground seashell mortar surviving since 1807. The aqueduct, uncovered alongside the Easton and Canyon Trail, is an archaeological relic that explains at once how Mission Santa Barbara, down the canyon, prospered on the strength of water and Indian converts. Indeed, the same pairing comes to mind in front of the church at the scoured stone laundry troughs, the *lavanderia* of 1816. Through bear-shaped spouts, as smooth and stylized as a Bufano sculpture, flowed the water from Mission Dam in the Botanic Garden.

AFTERWORD

 Whether it is human nature or a conditioned response to modern marketing methods, the sentiment "I want that" occurs to most people during a garden tour. In fact, the more the thought comes up, the more likely the visitor is to judge the garden a success. You can't take the garden home, but ideas and inspiration are useful souvenirs that can enhance your sojourn as well as your residential landscape.

Observe the difference between "landscaping" and "garden." Landscaping beautifies the built environment by introducing greenery and natural forms, and woe to us without it. But a garden is where the muse resides. Get a feel for the garden you are in. There is no other place just like it on earth. Ask yourself why, and bring the muse home for a stay.

Wherever your garden, whatever its size, the grand examples tell us this without equivocation: **begin with a strong design framework.** Traditional landscape design elements such as framed views, focal points, enclosure, sequence, and surprise can be utilized on the home front to ensure effective results. Developing a master plan is a valuable part of the design process but no guarantee that the design itself will be visually compelling. Use your artistry and powers of observation to organize the garden with flair, or consult a landscape architect.

Give your garden a purpose. The most engaging of public gardens are dedicated to a goal, and discovering how the goal is achieved, like following the plot in a story, is part of the pleasure in exploring them. At home, being purposeful does not constrain the freedom and joy to be found in working with plants but guides decision making, and gives the garden meaning. The objective may be as general as "garden color" or "outdoor room," or as precise as showcasing a horticultural collection. For membership in the American Association of Botanical Gardens and Arboreta, public gardens must adopt a mission statement, a form of guidance equally applicable to residential gardens. On a large property there may be room to pursue several avenues at once, but in a small-space garden elements that contribute to a single goal bestow a cohesive and peaceful quality.

Let your personal spirit shine. The best gardens are elevated above the ordinary or institutional by the vision and commitment of exceptional individuals. There is no garden without a person to tend it, which may explain the fascination gardens have held for writers since ancient Greece. Using the garden as an opportunity for self-expression and nurturing contributes directly to its strength.

Enlist help when you need it. Public gardens are maintained by teamwork: crews with rotating duty or perennial assignment to a given quadrant or task. Even if your garden is a low-key, leisure avocation and ostensibly not for display, there are times of the year when garden chores exceed the time allotted. Improve the way the garden looks and your enjoyment of it by drafting family members or hiring assistance when it is needed most.

Many of the public gardens are horticulturally enriched by plant species little seen or known elsewhere. At home, **have at least one truly rare or unusual plant specimen.** Few people can afford to purchase an antiquity or master's canvas, but nature's rarities and the distinction they confer can often be had for little more than the cost of regular attention. Shop at botanic garden plant sales, a tremendous resource for the curious gardener, or at smaller specialty nurseries that advertise in horticulture magazines. Your one of a kind, as the feature of a tour, can lure you and your companions into the garden room. A simple way to highlight the distinguishing features of your find is to grow its common cousins for comparison.

When you are thrilled by flower, foliage, or form in a public garden, **write down the name of the plant and its salient characteristics.** One thing the acquisitive can take with them is the accurate knowledge of the size and appearance of full-grown specimens, information unavailable in nurseries and hard to come by in books. Most public gardens try to keep up with labeling. (If there is no plaque, read the accession tag, an embossed aluminum strip with the scientific name, date of installation, and a call number that corresponds to an inventory maintained by garden staff.)

Be suggestive. Use individual plants, plant groupings, garden furnishings, or layouts that remind you of a cherished time and place. Almost any garden can remove you from the daily rush, but specific references are your passage to personal ports of call. Plants can be emissaries, originating at some distant point on the globe yet growing in your soil. Some Southern California gardens were started in just this way; others—the ones that you visit on holiday—can be the source of such allusion.

Finally, **provide a place to sit.** A public garden without a bench is unthinkable, yet many home gardens fail to offer this basic amenity. A seat in the garden beckons, and helps to make the garden at home a desired destination.

GEOGRAPHIC DIRECTORY OF GARDENS OPEN TO THE PUBLIC

The following directory is organized by county— Los Angeles, Orange, Riverside, San Diego, and Santa Barbara—each with its own map. Los Angeles County, with so many public gardens, is further divided into five geographic subareas. Under each heading, gardens featured in the text are listed first, in alphabetical order, followed by supplemental entries representing different types of gardens. Many of the latter lack the scope of the featured destinations, but by the same token they tend to be more focused and often more intimate.

Every effort was made to include in this list any public garden that inarguably qualifies as such. There are, however, many places that are gardenlike, having some but not all of the essential qualities, and others still that have gardens ancillary to their purpose, such as missions, campuses, urban plazas, museums, hotels, historic houses, retail nurseries, and nature preserves. These are not treated comprehensively by category. Rather, outstanding examples of the type are meant to suggest your further exploration in similar places. Discovering a garden is, after all, a good part of its pleasure.

Admission is free unless otherwise noted. "Nominal admission fee" means an entry charge of three dollars or less per adult. "Admission fee" denotes a charge in excess of that. Many gardens are available for wedding ceremonies by prearrangement. Most of the major gardens have a bookstore or gift shop, and most botanic gardens conduct plant sales.

Where zip codes do not appear, the addresses listed are for location only, not for mail.

Many gardens require advance reservations. This is generally a method to limit traffic through the residential areas in which the gardens are located.

We found that a hat with brim added greatly to our stamina and comfort in the gardens.

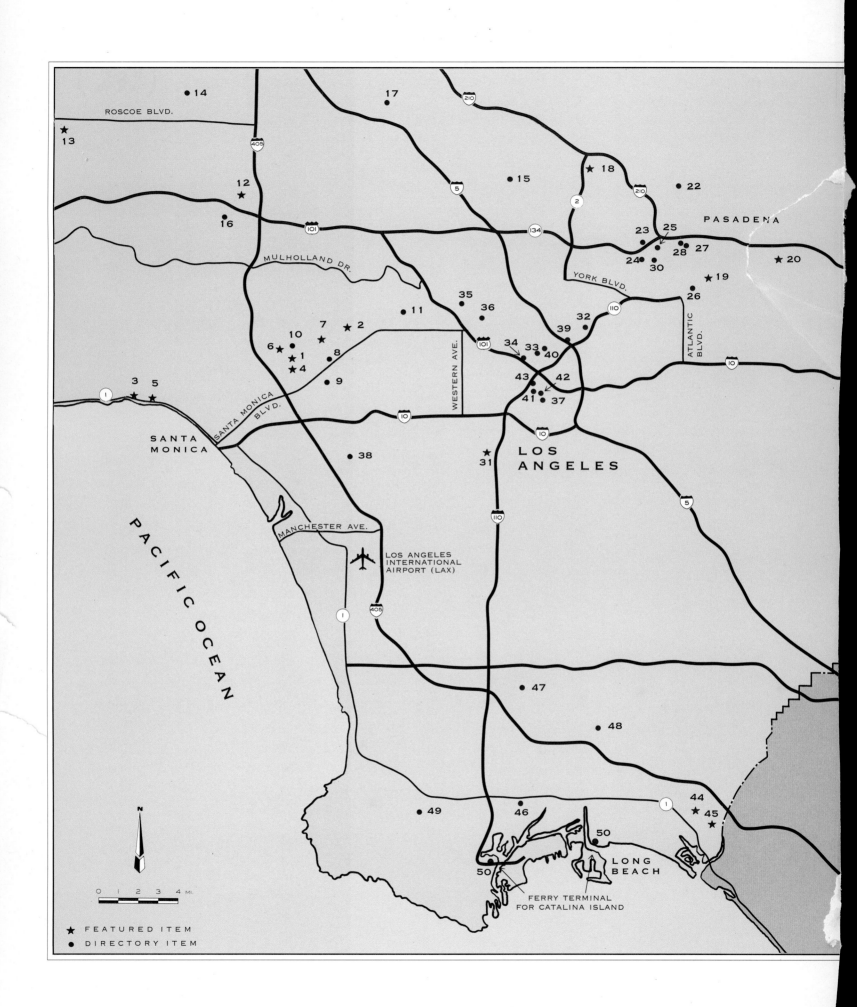

PACIFIC OCEAN

ROSCOE BLVD.

•14

17

•13

12

•15

★18

•22

PASADENA

•16

23 25

•24 •28 27

•30

MULHOLLAND DR.

YORK BLVD.

★20

★19

•26

•35

•36

•11

32

7

39

10

34 33 40

6 ★1

8

43 42

★4

9

41 37

3 5

SANTA MONICA BLVD.

WESTERN AVE.

ATLANTIC BLVD.

SANTA MONICA

•38

★31

LOS ANGELES

MANCHESTER AVE.

LOS ANGELES
INTERNATIONAL
AIRPORT (LAX)

•47

•48

•49

•46

44

★45

50

LONG BEACH

50

FERRY TERMINAL
FOR CATALINA ISLAND

N

0 1 2 3 4 MI.

★ FEATURED ITEM
• DIRECTORY ITEM

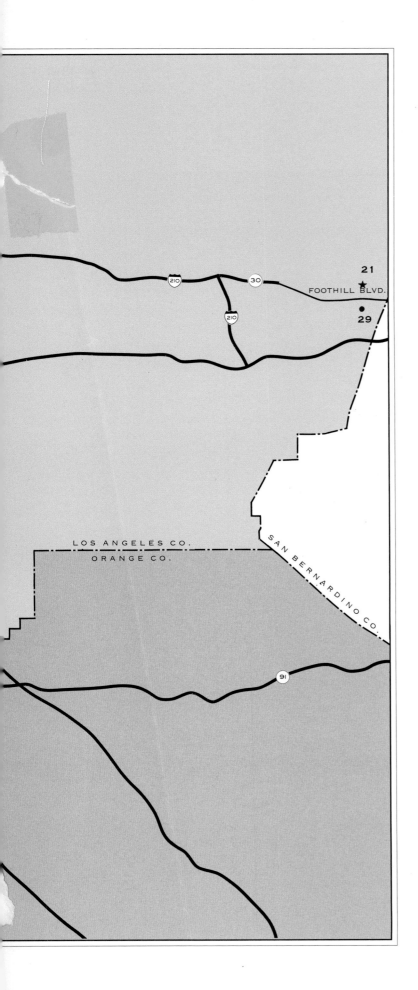

LOS ANGELES COUNTY

FEATURED GARDENS

1. **Franklin D. Murphy Sculpture Garden, UCLA**
University of California
Los Angeles, CA 90024
(Adjoins the Wight Art Gallery at the
    north end of the Westwood campus.)
213-825-9345

Open daily, day and night.
Parking fee on campus.

2. **Greystone Park**
905 Loma Vista Dr.
Beverly Hills, CA 90210
213-550-4654

Open daily:
Winter months, 10 A.M. to 5 P.M.
Summer months, 10 A.M. to 6 P.M.

3. **The J. Paul Getty Museum**
17985 Pacific Coast Highway
Malibu, CA 90265
213-458-2003

Tuesday through Sunday, 10 A.M. to 5 P.M.
Closed Mondays, New Year's Day, the
    Fourth of July, Thanksgiving Day,
    and Christmas Day.

Admission Policy: Under the terms of
    an agreement with local
    homeowners, it is the museum's
    responsibility to ensure that visitors
    do not park on surrounding streets.
    Therefore no walk-in traffic is
    permitted. Parking on museum
    premises is extremely limited, and is
    by advance reservation only.

For parking reservations, call or write the reservations office at the number above (seven days a week, 9 A.M. to 5 P.M.). It is advisable to call one week to ten days in advance of your visit. If parking reservations are unavailable, alternatives are either to be dropped off at the security kiosk by taxicab or automobile (evidence that you have not parked in the neighborhood) or to take the public transit bus (obtain free admission pass to the Getty from bus driver).

4. **The Mildred E. Mathias Botanical Garden, UCLA**
University of California
Los Angeles, CA 90024-1606
(Adjoins Mira Hershey Hall at the southwest corner of the Westwood campus.)
213-825-3620

Monday through Friday, 8 A.M. to 5 P.M.
Saturday and Sunday, 8 A.M. to 4 P.M.
Closed on university holidays.

5. **Self-Realization Fellowship Lake Shrine**
17190 Sunset Blvd.
Pacific Palisades, CA 90272
213-454-4114

Tuesday through Saturday, 9 A.M. to 4:45 P.M.
Sunday, 12:30 P.M. to 4:45 P.M.
Closed Mondays, holidays, and occasionally on Saturdays.

6. **The UCLA Hannah Carter Japanese Garden**
10619 Bellagio Rd.
Los Angeles, CA 90024
(Located in the town of Bel Air.)
Telephone UCLA Visitors' Center,
213-825-4574

Open by reservation only, during these hours:
Tuesday, 10 A.M. to 1 P.M.
Wednesday, noon to 3 P.M.

7. **Virginia Robinson Gardens**
1008 Elden Way
Beverly Hills, CA 90210
213-276-5367

Open for guided walking tours by appointment only. Visitors are not admitted without reservations.
Tours available Tuesday through Friday at 10 A.M. and 1 P.M.
Nominal admission fee.

ADDITIONAL GARDENS

8. **Cactus Garden**
Beverly Hills, CA
(On the north side of Santa Monica Blvd. between Camden Dr. and Bedford Dr.)
(No telephone.)

Open daily.

A glimpse of the desert from West L.A.'s major thoroughfare.

9. **Century Plaza Hotel and Tower**
2025 Avenue of the Stars
Los Angeles, CA 90067
213-277-2000

Open daily.

A swimming pool terrace garden, exemplary of 1960s modernism.

10. **Hotel Bel-Air**
    701 Stone Canyon Rd.
    Los Angeles, CA 90077
    213-472-1211

    Open daily.

    Sylvan and genteel; a variety of garden
    spaces, some bordering a meandering
    stream. Featuring several of L.A.'s
    most prestigious trees, including the
    floss-silk tree (largest in the U.S.) and
    the rare, blue-flowered lonchocharpus.
    Also an herb garden.

11. **Wattles Mansion and Garden**
    1850 N. Curson Ave.
    Los Angeles, CA 90046
    213-465-5993
    213-875-4005

    Open by appointment only, Monday
    through Friday 10 A.M. to 4 P.M.

    During the Golden Era, Oklahoman
    Gurdon Wattles wintered on a forty-
    nine-acre estate here, taking up
    permanent residence in 1922.
    Hollywood Heritage has commenced
    restoration of the derelict Mission
    Revival house (architects Hunt and
    Grey, 1907) and formal gardens on
    four remaining acres, beginning with
    the Italianate terraces and an antique
    rose garden on the hillside. A teahouse
    in the adjoining city park is a reminder
    of an oriental landscape motif,
    elsewhere on the original property and
    long gone.

FEATURED GARDENS

12. **Donald C. Tillman Water
    Reclamation Plant Japanese
    Garden**
    6100 Woodley Ave.
    Van Nuys, CA 91406
    818-989-8166

    Entry to the garden is by conducted
    tour only; tours conducted on
    Tuesday, Thursday, and Saturday
    mornings.
    Call for reservation.

13. **Orcutt Ranch Horticulture Center**
    23600 Roscoe Blvd.
    West Hills, CA 91304
    818-883-6641

    Open daily, 8 A.M. to 5 P.M.
    Closed major holidays.

ADDITIONAL GARDENS

14. **California State University,
    Northridge Botanical Garden**
    18111 Nordhoff St.
    Northridge, CA 91330
    818-885-3496

    Monday through Friday, 8 A.M. to 5 P.M.

    Small garden used by the Biology
    Department.

15. **Friendship Garden**
1601 W. Mountain St.
Glendale, CA 91201
(In Brand Park.)
818-956-2147

Monday through Friday, 10 A.M. to 3 P.M.

An expression of amity between
Higashi Osaka and Glendale. Sister
cities' Japanese gardens are well
distributed in Southern California.

16. **Sepulveda Garden Center**
16633 Magnolia Blvd.
Encino, CA 91316
818-784-5180

Open daily, 7 A.M. to 3:30 P.M.
Closed major holidays.

A cornucopia of garden plots. With
375 of them consuming approximately
eight acres, "you can see the same
thing grown a hundred different ways,"
one staff member told me. As popular
with observers as with participants.

17. **The Theodore Payne Foundation
for Wildflowers and Native Plants**
10459 Tuxford St.
Sun Valley, CA 91352
818-768-1802

Tuesday through Saturday, 8:30 A.M.
to 4:30 P.M.

A place of pilgrimage for lovers of
native flora. California hillsides alive
with wildflowers to admire or purchase.
Theodore Payne was the first to
perceive and popularize the untapped
resource of indigenous plants,
beginning in 1903. By the time of his
retirement in 1961, at age ninety, he
had introduced 430 species into
cultivation. The foundation carries on
his work.

FEATURED GARDENS

18. **Descanso Gardens**
1418 Descanso Dr.
La Cañada Flintridge, CA 91011
818-790-5571

Open daily, 9 A.M. to 5 P.M.
Closed Christmas Day.
Nominal admission fee.
Free admission third Tuesday of each
month.

19. **The Huntington Library, Art
Collections, and Botanical Gardens**
1151 Oxford Rd.
San Marino, CA 91108
818-405-2100

Tuesday through Sunday, 1 P.M. to 4:30 P.M.
Closed Mondays and major holidays.
Advance reservations required for
Sundays: call 818-405-2141.

20. **Los Angeles State and County
Arboretum**
301 N. Baldwin Ave.
Arcadia, CA 91007-2697
818-446-8251

Open daily , 9 A.M. to 5 P.M., except:
Tropical Greenhouse: daily, 10 A.M. to 3 P.M.
Begonia Greenhouse: Monday through
Friday, 9 A.M. to 3 P.M.
Plant Science Library: Monday
through Friday, 9 A.M. to 4:30 P.M.
Closed Christmas Day.

21. **Rancho Santa Ana Botanic Garden**
1500 N. College Ave.
Claremont, CA 91711-3101
714-625-8767

Open daily, 8:00 A.M. to 5:00 P.M.
Closed New Year's Day, the Fourth of
  July, Thanksgiving, Christmas Day.

22. **Christmas Tree Lane**
Santa Rosa St. between Woodbury and
  Mariposa in Altadena
(No mailing address or telephone.)

Illuminated between Christmas Day
  and New Year's Day.

In 1885, John Woodbury brought back
from India seeds of the now-ubiquitous
deodor cedar, and planted them in two
straight rows on his nine-hundred-acre
rancho. He never built a home there,
just a platform to watch the trees grow.
The custom of lighting the monumental
deodors, begun in the 1920s, is
continued by neighborhood residents.
(Some trees are missing.)

23. **Gamble House**
4 Westmoreland Pl.
Pasadena, CA 91103
818-793-3334

Grounds open daily.
(House open Thursday through
  Sunday, noon to 3 P.M.)

Renowned as the ultimate expression of
the Craftsman esthetic (architects
Greene and Greene, 1908), the house
wouldn't sing without the artful setting.
The ground is carefully contoured,
anticipating the landscape berming now
used commonly in California. Inspired
brickwork.

24. **La Casita de Arroyo**
177 S. Arroyo Blvd.
Pasadena, CA 91105
(No telephone.)

Gardens always open.

Adjoining an arroyo stone park
building (1932), a new, drought-
tolerant demonstration garden shows
the effects of differing amounts of
water on three plantings. Conservation
also extends to other landscape
features, such as porous paving in the
parking lot. Designed by landscape
architect Isabelle Greene; sponsored
and maintained by the Pasadena
Garden Club.

25. **Norton Simon Museum**
411 W. Colorado Blvd.
Pasadena, CA 91105
818-449-6840

Thursday through Sunday, noon to
  6 P.M.
Closed New Year's Day, Thanksgiving,
  Christmas Day.
Nominal admission fee.

The strongest element in this sculpture
garden is the long, formal pool, a slick
black plane reflecting the geometry of
the museum wings that enclose it. The
courtyard extends and illuminates
galleries and lobby. Powerful torsos and
abstract forms by the modern masters,
including Rodin, Moore, Maillol, and
Laurens.

26. **The Old Mill**
"El Molino Viejo"
1120 Old Mill Rd.
San Marino, CA 91108
818-449-5450

Open daily except Monday and
holidays, 1 P.M. to 4 P.M.

Agave and citrus, loquat and sycamore
join an ancient gnarled peach tree in
the romantic walled garden of the grist
mill that served the Mission San
Gabriel Arcangel, agriculturally the
richest of the California missions. The
tile-roofed adobe is a composition of
warm-hued plaster, timber lintels, and
climbing roses. An intimate antidote to
the Huntington gardens, a few minutes'
drive away.

27. **Pacific Asia Museum**
46 N. Los Robles Ave.
Pasadena, CA 91101
818-449-2742

Wednesday through Sunday, noon to 5 P.M.
Nominal admission fee to galleries.
Free, third Saturday of every month.

A tranquil courtyard fully contained by
the former gallery and residence of
Asian-art collector Grace Nicholson,
built in the Chinese Imperial Palace
style in the 1920s. Good-sized gingkos,
a golden rain tree, Chinese magnolias,
koi, and lion dogs from the Ch'ing
Dynasty authenticate the scene. Only
the emperor's nightingale is missing.
One of the few Chinese courtyard
gardens in the U.S.

28. **Pasadena City Hall**
100 N. Garfield Ave.
Pasadena, CA 91101
818-405-4222

Courtyard always open.

The place to experience Beaux Arts
classicism. The towers and arcades of
Bakewell and Brown's 1925 civic
structure enclose a refined courtyard
with a central fountain the equal of
many in Europe. Claim a sunny or tree-
shaded bench to enjoy seasonal color,
the sound of water, and an urbane
setting unusual in Los Angeles.

29. **Pomona College**
333 N. College Way
Claremont, CA 91711
714-621-8146

Gardens always open.

A succession of large and small spaces
worthy of exploration, some of them
designed by landscape architect Ralph
Cornell, demonstrates the virtues that
good landscape design can bring to a
campus, and the campus can bring to a
community.

30. **Tournament House and Wrigley
Gardens**
(William Wrigley, Jr., Mansion)
391 S. Orange Grove Blvd.
Pasadena, CA 91184
818-449-4100

Gardens open daily, except December 31
and New Year's Day.
(House open February through September
on Wednesday, 2 P.M. to 4 P.M.)

Two display gardens of All-America Rose Selections winners, and one champion fig tree. A curved pergola defines a wedding site and adds a grace note to heroic expanses of palm-studded lawn.

CENTRAL AND
EAST LOS ANGELES

FEATURED GARDEN

31. **Exposition Park Rose Garden**
900 Exposition Blvd.
Los Angeles, CA 90007
213-548-7671

Open daily, sunrise to sunset.

ADDITIONAL GARDENS

32. **Charles F. Lummis Home and Garden**
"El Alisal"
200 E. Avenue 43
Los Angeles, CA 90031
213-222-0546

Thursday through Sunday, 1 P.M. to 4 P.M. Tours at other times by appointment.

Charles Lummis, mission enthusiast and founder of the Southwest Museum in Los Angeles, built his house of local arroyo stone and heavy timbers. Now the headquarters of the Historical Society of Southern California, it forms a suitable backdrop for the drought-tolerant native plantings that compose the garden and demonstrate

that color and greenery are not exclusive to water-thirsty planting plans. Robert Perry, landscape architect.

33. **Chavez Ravine Arboretum**
Los Angeles, CA
(In L.A.'s Elysian Park, on Stadium Way from Scott Ave. to Academy Rd.)
213-485-5054

Open daily, sunrise to sunset.

The remnant of a late-nineteenth-century arboretum with many notable trees.

34. **Echo Park Lotus Pond**
Glendale Blvd. and Park Ave.
Los Angeles, CA 90026
213-485-5054

Open daily.

Go in summer to see the lotus in bloom.

35. **Fern Dell**
Los Angeles, CA
(In Griffith Park, on Ferndell Dr. between Black Oak Dr. and Red Oak Dr.)
213-665-5188

Open daily, sunrise to sunset.

The streamside environment and arching canopy of alder, redwood, and sycamore provide the perfect growing conditions for a fern collection. A cool summer retreat.

36. **Hollyhock House**
Barnsdall Park
4800 Hollywood Blvd.
Los Angeles, CA 90027
213-662-7272

Tuesday through Thursday,
10 A.M. to 1 P.M.
Saturdays and the first three Sundays
each month, noon to 3 p.m.
Nominal admission fee.

The interior courtyard and grounds of
Frank Lloyd Wright's Mayan-inspired
residence (1921) for oil heiress Aline
Barnsdall.

37. **James Irvine Garden**
Japanese American Cultural and
Community Center
244 S. San Pedro St.
Los Angeles, CA 90012
213-628-2725

Open daily, 9 A.M. to 5 P.M.
Closed holidays.

The soul of Little Tokyo. A carefully
wrought garden commemorating
Japanese heritage. Called Seiryu-en,
"Garden of the Clear Stream."

38. **Kaizuka Meditation Garden**
Culver City Library
4975 Overland Ave.
Culver City, CA 90230
213-559-1676

Open daily.

Zen on the run. A condensed,
streetside Japanese garden in lieu of
foundation shrubs.

39. **Lawry's California Center**
570 W. Avenue 26
Los Angeles, CA 90065
213-224-6850

Gardens open daily, 11 A.M. to 9 P.M.
Restaurants open daily, 11 A.M. to
3 P.M. for lunch, 4:30 P.M. to
10 P.M. for dinner.
Gardens and restaurants closed New
Year's Day, Thanksgiving,
Christmas Day.

This Los Angeles seasoning company
has seized the promotional value of
California garden imagery. Popular
restaurant ramadas overlook a densely
planted patio garden, bursting with
floral color, fountains, banners,
azulejos, flowering trees, and a dash of
Old Mexico. Twinkling lights and
mariachis give the patio a nighttime
dimension unavailable at most public
gardens.

40. **Los Angeles Police Academy**
1880 N. Academy Rd.
Los Angeles, CA 90012
213-222-9136
213-485-3151

Open by appointment only.

Well-guarded hillside rock garden.

41. **MOCA—The Museum of
Contemporary Art**
250 S. Grand Ave.
Los Angeles, CA 90012
(At California Plaza.)
213-626-6222

Plaza open daily.
(Museum open Tuesday through
Sunday, 11 A.M. to 6 P.M., except
Thursday open until 8 P.M.
Admission fee to museum.)

Complementing the disciplined architecture (1986) of Arata Isozaki, which steals the show from the art within, a dynamic postmodern plaza. Sumptuous materials.

42. **The New Otani Hotel and Garden**
120 S. Los Angeles St.
Los Angeles, CA 90012
213-629-1200

Open daily, day and night.

An unexpected venue many stories above Los Angeles for waterfalls, azaleas, full-sized trees, and sacred stones. See L.A. City Hall from Tokyo. Garden adjoins two restaurants.

43. **Union Bank Square**
445 S. Figueroa St.
Los Angeles, CA 90071
213-236-7468

Open daily.

A crisp composition, the elements neatly separated. Trees, turf, and blue mosaic fountain are raised islands in a concrete paving grid. A classic downtown plaza designed by landscape architect Garrett Eckbo (1968).

NOTE: Although listed in other guidebooks, the scent garden for the blind in Lafayette Park has been reduced to a few bedraggled plants in dusty beds, and is neither aromatic nor gardenesque. The park, on the other hand, has become the pulsating center of community life for its Hispanic neighborhood.

FEATURED GARDENS

44. **Earl Burns Miller Japanese Garden**
California State University, Long Beach
Long Beach, CA 90840
(On Earl Warren Dr.)
213-985-8885

Tuesday through Thursday, 9 A.M. to 4 P.M. (during daylight savings time, until 5 P.M.)
Sunday, noon to 4 P.M.

45. **Rancho Los Alamitos**
6400 Bixby Hill Rd.
Long Beach, CA 90815
213-431-3541

Wednesday through Sunday, 1 P.M. to 5 P.M.
Closed holidays.
Special tours by appointment.

ADDITIONAL GARDENS

46. **Banning Residence Museum**
401 E. M St.
Wilmington, CA 90744
213-548-7777

Park open daily.
(House tours Tuesday through Sunday, 12:30 P.M. to 2:30 P.M.)

The grounds of Gen. Phineas Banning's Greek Revival residence have assumed the character of a city park. Eucalyptus and an enormous wisteria are part of Banning's garden legacy. Note the cast iron fence with cornstalk motif.

47. **Japanese Friendship Garden**
California State University,
   Dominguez Hills
1000 E. Victoria St.
Carson, CA 90747
213-516-3804

Open daily.

A small atrium garden called Shin-
wa-en, "an island dominated by
mountains and forests."

48. **Rancho Los Cerritos**
4600 Virginia Rd.
Long Beach, CA 90807
213-424-9423

Wednesday through Sunday, 1 P.M. to 5 P.M.
Closed major holidays.

An adobe ranch house built by
Jonathon Temple in 1844 occupies the
five remaining acres of his original
twenty-seven thousand. Cypress spires
from Temple's Italianate garden
survive.

49. **South Coast Botanic Garden**
26300 Crenshaw Blvd.
Palos Verdes Peninsula, CA 90274
213-377-0468

Open daily, 9 A.M. to 5 P.M., except
   Christmas Day.
Nominal admission fee.

The site of an open pit mine, later a
landfill, now, incredibly, a botanic
garden. In addition to the standard
practice of grouping plants by family,
theme gardens by color (blue, pink,
yellow) have been installed.

50. **Wrigley Memorial and Botanical
Garden**
1400 Avalon Canyon Rd.
Avalon, CA 90704
(Ferries for Catalina Island embark
   from Long Beach and San Pedro;
   tram service from downtown Avalon
   connects to the botanic garden.)
213-510-2288

Open daily, 8 A.M. to 5 P.M.
Closed holidays.
Nominal admission fee.

A garden underwritten by the chewing
gum heirs to preserve and study the
native flora of the Channel Islands,
which support approximately 100
species, subspecies, and varieties
unique to that location. On the islands,
some plants exhibit surprising
tendencies compared to mainland kin,
such as gigantism and near-perpetual
bloom. Others are extremely rare; of
Catalina mahogany only five trees
remain in the wild.

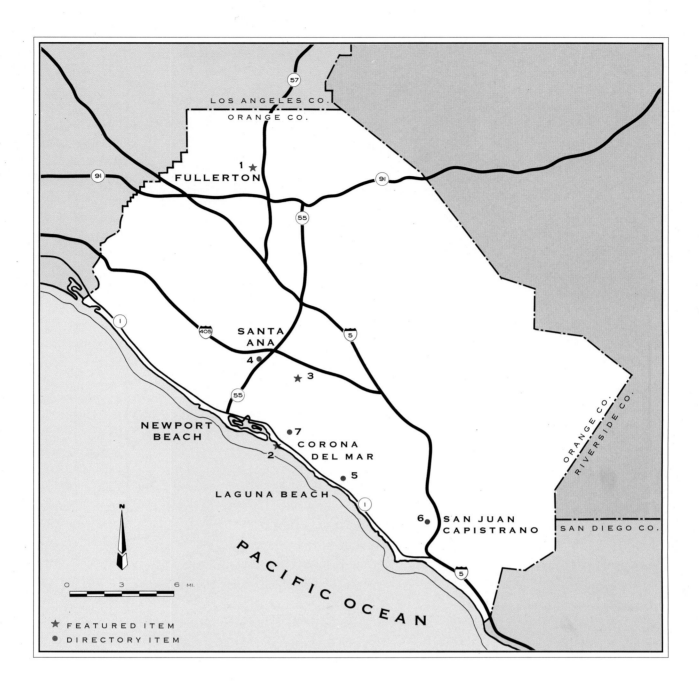

ORANGE COUNTY

1. **Fullerton Arboretum**
   California State University, Fullerton
   Fullerton, CA 92634
   (On the northeast corner of campus;
     entrance is from Associated Rd.)
   714-773-3579

   Open daily, 8 A.M. to 4:45 P.M.
   Closed New Year's Day, Thanksgiving,
     Christmas Day.

2. **Sherman Library and Gardens**
   2647 E. Pacific Coast Hwy.
   Corona del Mar, CA 92625
   714-673-2261

   Open daily, 10:30 A.M. to 4:00 P.M.
   Nominal admission fee.

3. **UC Irvine Arboretum**
University of California
Irvine, CA 92717
(Entrance on Campus Dr., east of
Jamboree Rd.)
714-856-5833

Monday through Friday, 8:30 A.M. to
3:30 P.M.
Closed Saturday, Sunday, and all
federal holidays.

ADDITIONAL GARDENS

4. **California Scenario**
South Coast Plaza Town Center
Costa Mesa, CA 92626
(San Diego Freeway at Bristol St.)
714-241-1700

Open daily, 7 A.M. to midnight.

Sculptor Isamu Noguchi's symbolic
summing up of California's
environment, 1982. A plane of
thick sandstone slabs, pierced to
reveal a watercourse, brings the
expansiveness of nature to a corporate
plaza and provides a stage for abstract,
sculptural tableaux. Wear sunglasses.

5. **Hortense Miller Garden**
Laguna Beach, CA
714-497-3311

By escorted tour only.
Monday and Friday; hours by arrangement.
Contact City of Laguna Beach two
weeks in advance at above number.

Privileged view of a plantswoman's
home garden.

6. **Mission San Juan Capistrano**
San Juan Capistrano, CA 92675
(On Interstate 5.)
714-493-1111

Open daily, 7:30 A.M. to 5 P.M.

In the early twentieth century, mission
courtyards were spruced up for
tourism, planted with flowers to make
the antiquity an appealing roadside
attraction. A landscape of trees and
roses around Father Serra's church
(the oldest building in California) is
among the better make-overs of that
period.

7. **Roger's Gardens**
Newport Center
2301 San Joaquin Hills Rd.
Corona del Mar, CA 92625
(At MacArthur.)
714-640-5800

Open daily:
April 1 through Oct. 20: 9 A.M. to 6 P.M.
Oct. 21 through Dec. 30: 9 A.M. to 9 P.M.,
except Sunday to 6 P.M.
Jan. 1 through March 31: 9 A.M. to 5 P.M.
Closed Thanksgiving, Christmas Day,
New Year's Day.

A retail nursery verging on amusement
park. A bonanza of color, a good
source for how-to advice, and the place
to buy mock topiary elephants or
reindeer. Not for the indecisive.

NOTE: At Disneyland,
Orange County's gift to
the world, the illusion
would not be complete
without generous land-
scaping adroitly arranged.
The fantasy settings and
streetscapes depend upon
garden elements for ver-
isimilitude and psychologi-
cal comfort; plants are the
touchstone that make fab-
ricated environments seem
real.

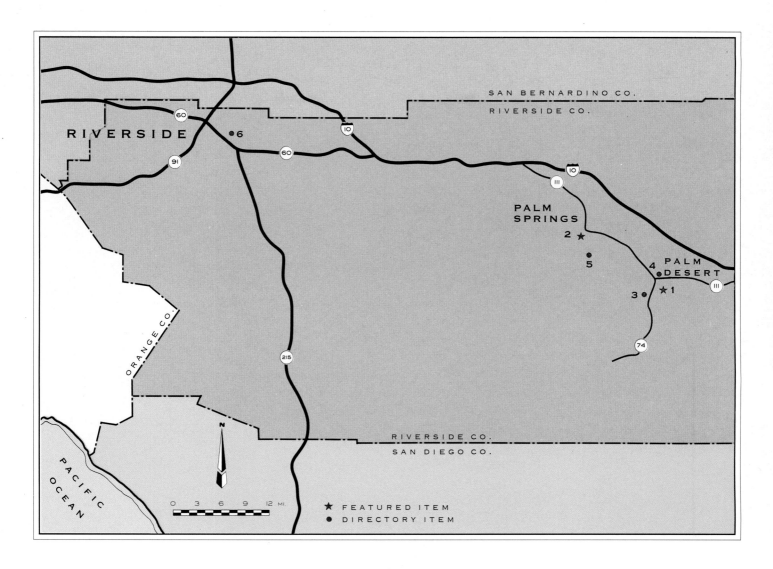

RIVERSIDE COUNTY

FEATURED GARDENS

1. **The Living Desert**
   47-900 Portola
   Palm Desert, CA 92260
   619-346-5694

   Open daily, 9 A.M. to 5 P.M.
   (Last admission, 4:30 P.M.)
   Closed June 16 through August 31.
   Admission fee.

2. **Moorten Botanical Garden**
   1701 South Palm Canyon Dr.
   Palm Springs, CA 92264
   619-327-6555

Monday through Saturday, 9 A.M. to
   4:30 P.M.
Sunday, 10 A.M. to 4 P.M.
Nominal admission fee.

ADDITIONAL GARDENS

3. **Aerie Sculpture Garden and
   Gallery**
   71-225 Aerie Dr.
   Palm Desert, CA 92260
   619-568-6366

Friday through Monday, 1 P.M. to 4 P.M.
Other days by appointment at your convenience.
Nominal admission fee.

A real find. Artists Bruce and Clonard Thomas are creating a brand new garden in the scenic desert foothills, a personal expression featuring their own work and that of selected colleagues. The sculpture is animated by desert light that seems to come from all directions. A molded wing of transparent plexiglass called "Clear Sail" by Bruce Thomas, for example, intensifies the mood of the sky. Fine assortment of plants named and illustrated on glazed ceramic plaques. Relaxation invited, artwork for sale.

4. **College of the Desert Arboretum**
42500 Monterey Ave.
Palm Desert, CA 92260
619-346-8041

Open daily.

On campus and adjoining City Hall, an effort to expand the plant palette for the Coachella Valley by demonstrating desert-tested trees from other geographic regions.

5. **Palm Canyon**
38-520 S. Palm Canyon Dr.
Palm Springs, CA 92263
619-325-5673

Open daily, 8:00 A.M. to 5 P.M.
Nominal admission fee.

Certain California trees have long been recognized for their landscape value, and, so used, have a characteristic look. This is nothing like the character conveyed when these familiar figures appear in native stands. Gathered among their own kind, the trees define a unique, almost hallowed place, their signature features exaggerated by separation and sheer number. In this sheltered canyon the California fan palms convene around a desert stream, bestowing a gardenlike quality. Rare in the wild, this palm was introduced to mission gardens by the padres and has since become a fixture in Southern California. But unlike the straifed poles we know as their trunks, California fan palms in their original habitat wear a skirt of thatch almost to the ground.

Admission entitles you also to visit Andreas Canyon and Murray Canyon, like Palm Canyon on the tribal lands of the Agua Caliente Indians.

6. **UC Riverside Botanic Gardens**
University of California
Riverside, CA 92521
(Follow Campus Dr. to Parking Lot 13 to reach the Botanic Gardens parking area.)
714-787-4650

Open daily, 8 A.M. to 5 P.M.
Closed New Year's Day, Fourth of July, Thanksgiving, Christmas Day.

The equal of many of the featured gardens in scope, pleasure, and scientific purpose, the UC Riverside Botanic Gardens are beautifully sited in a bowl of the Box Spring Mountains, and borrow their rugged scenery. The diverse terrain (arroyos, hillsides, and a 350-foot elevation change) enlivens the walk and provides growing conditions for diverse plant collections on nearly forty acres, including an enchanted grove of fig trees. Amble through a cool alder glade and emerge on a sunny plateau with iris, rose, and herb gardens, or head off to the plant family and Australian sections. Roadrunners act as escort.

NOTE: If you're looking for the agricultural landscape of Southern California, Riverside County is a good bet, at least for now. (Here, too, farmland is disappearing rapidly.) Early packing-crate labels depicted rows of orange trees vanishing into the horizon, and in Riverside the grand palm-lined boulevard of Victoria Avenue led to such plantations. On the perimeter of that city extensive orange groves can still be found. (UC Riverside runs a citrus experiment station). In Palm Desert and environs, farms of date palms, locally known as date "gardens," persist on the bustling commercial highway. Further south in Indio, date culture plays a large part in the local economy.

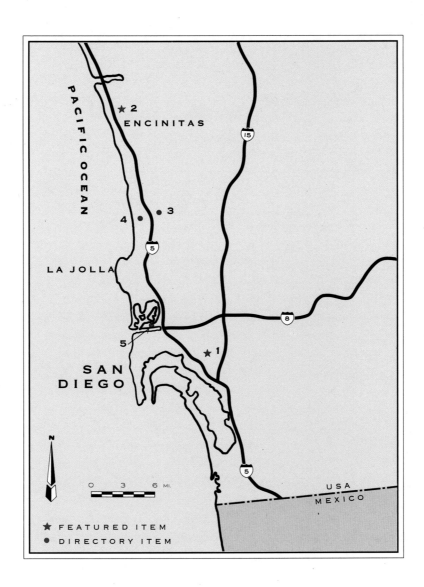

SAN DIEGO COUNTY

FEATURED GARDENS

1. **Balboa Park**
   City of San Diego Park and Recreation
   Department
   San Diego, CA 92101
   (The park itself is situated in the
   northeast quadrant of downtown
   San Diego.)
   619-236-5472

   Botanical Building:
   Open daily except Monday, 10 A.M. to
   4 P.M.

   Closed New Year's Day, Thanksgiving,
   Christmas Day.
   Lily Pond, Alcazar, Palm Canyon, Rose
   Garden, Desert Garden, Historic
   Garden at the Marston House
   Open daily.

   Free horticultural walking tour with
   four rotating themes every Saturday
   at 10 A.M.; meet in front of the
   Botanical Building.

San Diego Zoo
P.O. Box 5511
San Diego, CA 92112-0551
(In Balboa Park; entrance from
    Park Blvd.)
619-234-3153
619-231-1515

Open daily.
July through Labor Day, 9 A.M. to
    5 P.M.
Post–Labor Day through June, 9 A.M.
    to 4 P.M.
Admission fee.
Orchid open house, third Friday each
    month.
Botanical walk, by reservation,
    conducted by Offshoot Tours on the
    last Sunday of the month at 9:30
    A.M. Free with zoo admission or
    membership. 619-297-0289.

2. **Quail Botanical Gardens**
    230 Quail Gardens Dr.
    Encinitas, CA 92024
    619-436-3036: Foundation Office,
        11 A.M. to 1 P.M. Tuesday and
        Thursday
    619-436-8301: Herbarium
    619-753-4432: Ranger Station

    Open daily, 8 A.M. to 5 P.M., including
        holidays.
    Gift shop open Wednesday through
        Sunday, 11 A.M. to 3 P.M.
    Nominal fee for parking.

ADDITIONAL GARDENS

3. **Naiman Tech Center Japanese
    Garden**
    9605 Scranton Rd.
    San Diego, CA 92121
    619-453-9550

Open daily.

Bamboo hedge mirrored in a reflective
glass curtain wall, and other junctions
of Japanese garden art with an upscale
office complex. Takes mounding to new
heights.

4. **Salk Institute**
    10010 N. Torrey Pines Rd.
    La Jolla, CA 92037
    619-453-4100

    Monday through Friday, 8 A.M. to
        5 P.M.
    (The outdoor space can be seen but
        not entered when the gates are
        closed.)

    A masterpiece of landscape
    composition rendered largely in
    concrete by a master of modern
    architecture, Louis I. Kahn. Sky and
    sea merge seamlessly at the end of a
    powerfully framed vista.

5. **Sea World**
    1720 S. Shore Rd.
    Mission Bay Park
    San Diego, CA 92109
    619-226-3901

    Open daily.
    Summer: 9 A.M. to 11 P.M. Remainder
        of year: 9 A.M. to 5 P.M.
    Admission fee.

    While incidental to marine shows,
    exhibits, and aquariums that will devour
    your attention, the gardens of Sea
    World are nonetheless a miracle. Built
    on a former salt marsh, buffeted by
    strong prevailing winds, and battling a
    permanent salt water level as close as
    ten feet from the soil surface, the
    gardens support more than two
    thousand kinds of plants by applying
    defensive horticultural techniques.

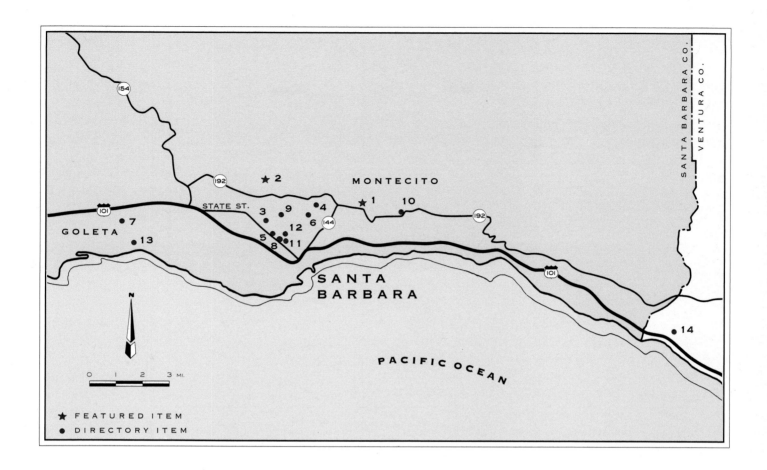

SANTA BARBARA COUNTY

1. **Lotusland**
   695 Ashley Rd.
   Santa Barbara, CA 93108
   805-969-3767

   Open by advance reservation only to groups with a horticultural or botanic affiliation. All visits are escorted, and drive-up entry without appointment is not permitted. Inquire regarding the current status of admission policy; regular hours for guided tours are planned.

2. **Santa Barbara Botanic Garden**
   1212 Mission Canyon Rd.
   Santa Barbara, CA 93105
   805-682-4726

Garden open daily, 8 A.M. to sunset.
Garden Shop open daily, 10 A.M. to 4 P.M.
Garden Growers Nursery open Tuesday, Thursday, Friday, and Saturday, 10 A.M. to 3 P.M.; Sunday, 11 A.M. to 3 P.M.
Reference Library and Herbarium open by appointment.

ADDITIONAL GARDENS

3. **Alice Keck Park Memorial Gardens**
   Garden St. at Micheltorena St.
   Santa Barbara, CA
   805-564-5433

Open daily.

A joyful place: 4.6 acres actively used for everything from sunbathing to Sunday outings, but above all, a new and colorful horticultural garden. Pond and streams designed for water interest. Plants identified by location on central kiosk.

4. **City of Santa Barbara Firescapes Demonstration Garden**
Mission Ridge at Stanwood Dr.
Santa Barbara, CA
(Across from Fire Station #7.)
805-965-5254

Open daily.

Surveying the beauty of the Santa Ynez Mountains from this well-tended garden, you can also sense the danger that wildfire poses to surrounding homes. Homeowners are advised to grow concentric zones of progressively fire resistant yet attractive plants, and the garden is arranged accordingly. Color-coded labels reinforce the message.

5. **El Paseo**
15 E. De la Guerra St.
Santa Barbara, CA 93101
805-965-0093

Courtyards open daily.

Why is Santa Barbara's downtown different from that of other cities? Because of places like El Paseo (1923), where intimate pedestrian passages weave through patios to shops and eateries behind the main street. Wend your way to Casa de la Guerra (1827), where the space opens up into the commandant's courtyard, surrounded on three sides by a covered walkway. This building and other nearby adobes lend authenticity to Santa Barbara's Spanish Colonial theme.

6. **Franceschi Park**
Franceschi Rd.
Santa Barbara, CA
(Off Mission Ridge Rd.)
805-564-5433

Open daily.

At the turn of the century, the incredible Florentine nobleman Francesco Franceschi introduced nine hundred plants and offered some two thousand choices at his nursery, while in residence at this hilltop estate called Montarioso. Although the property is practically derelict now, many unusual trees and shrubs survive (with stamped metal name tags), and time has not diminished the view over Santa Barbara and the Channel Islands. A garden of untapped potential.

7. **Goleta Water District Drought Tolerant Demonstration Garden**
Corner of Hollister Ave. and
    Puente Dr.
Goleta, CA
805-967-8605

Open daily.

Water-conserving landscape ideas for conscientious gardeners.

8. **La Arcada Court**
114 State St.
Santa Barbara, CA 93101
(No telephone.)

Open daily.

Romanticized Spanish shopping arcade with garden elements: flowers, fountain, flags, tiles, canopies, clock— the works.

9. **Mission Santa Barbara**
2201 Laguna St.
Santa Barbara, CA 93105
805-682-4713

Open daily, 9 A.M. to 5 P.M.
Nominal admission fee for adults.
   Children under sixteen admitted
   free.

Chalky pink domes surmount the most famous facade among California missions, set off by an expansive foreground of lawn. In contrast, behind the mission walls is a verdant courtyard enclosed by an arcade, with central fountain and a circle of California fan palms. The clerics who abided by the mission churches after secularization in 1834 planted the courtyards for sustenance and pleasure. (They were previously work yards.) The patio garden at Mission Santa Barbara dates from about 1840 and, according to garden historian Thomas A. Brown, is the best surviving example in close to original form.

Rose garden at the far end of the lawn, across the street.

10. **Montecito Water District Drought Tolerant Demonstration Garden**
583 San Ysidro Rd.
Santa Barbara, CA 93108
805-969-2271

A thoughtful layout illustrates the potential for esthetic satisfaction when growing the most sensible plants for a semiarid climate.

11. **Presidio Gardens**
122 E. Canon Perdido St.
Santa Barbara, CA 93101
805-966-9719

Open daily.

Not a period garden, but pleasant in its own right. Shade trees, fountain, koi.

12. **Santa Barbara County Courthouse**
1100 block of Anacapa St.
Santa Barbara, CA 93101
805-962-6464

Grounds open daily.
(Courthouse open Monday through
   Friday, 8 A.M. to 5 P.M.; Saturday
   and Sunday, 9 A.M. to 5 P.M.)

A popular fantasy from Moorish Spain, the ornate building (1929) embraces a sunken garden of lawn. Palms heighten the air of exoticism, and large conifers are in scale with the huge edifice.

13. **Santa Barbara Orchid Estate**
1250 Orchid Dr.
Santa Barbara, CA 93111
805-967-1284

Monday through Saturday, 8 A.M. to
   4:30 P.M.
Sunday, 11 A.M. to 4 P.M.
Closed holidays.

Situated in wholesale-nursery territory. Seaborne moisture creates the perfect environment for orchid culture, and every imaginable variety is grown in these vast enclosures. Breathtaking at peak bloom in March and April.

14. **Seaside Banana Garden**
6823 Santa Barbara Ave.
La Conchita-Ventura, CA 93001
(At the end of the Hwy. 101 frontage
    road at the Santa Barbara Ave. exit.)
805-643-4061

Open daily, March through November.
Open weekends only, December
    through February.
Tours by appointment, but an
    unescorted walk around a close-in
    banana grove is permitted on
    request.

On an unusually sheltered acreage
by the sea (said to be ten degrees
warmer at night than anywhere else
in the state), an amazing fifty varieties
of banana trees are producing a
luscious crop in this brand-new
enterprise. A symbol of the tropics
brought to fruition in California at long
last. Technically in Ventura County,
one mile south of the Santa Barbara
County line.

NOTES: There are many
outstanding private gar-
dens in Santa Barbara and
Montecito that are occa-
sionally open by special
arrangement for scholarly
research, fund raising
events, and the like. One
such is Casa del Herrero,
also known as the Medora
Bass Estate. For informa-
tion, contact the Founda-
tion for Santa Barbara City
College, 721 Cliff Drive,
Santa Barbara, CA 93109
(phone 805-965-0581).
Another means of entrée
to private gardens is to
attend the annual garden
tour conducted by Santa
Barbara Beautiful. For
particulars, phone
805-965-8867.

The importance of land-
scape design to the com-
munity of Santa Barbara is
underscored by the bronze
plaque in the center of
town in memory of land-
scape architect Lockwood
de Forest and his wife,
horticulturist and coeditor
of *Santa Barbara Garden*
Elizabeth de Forest.
(Located in front of the
Museum of Art at the
corner of State Street and
Anapamu Street.)

ACKNOWLEDGMENTS

I wish to thank all the people who very generously woke themselves up earlier than usual or gave their time into evening hours or on holidays for the photo sessions. I also would like to express my gratitude to those at Chronicle Books whose competence and good taste I can always count on, and special thanks to my editor Nion McEvoy for his enthusiastic support. And finally, many thanks to the gardeners and directors whose hard work and imagination created these gardens, making it possible for millions of visitors to enjoy and appreciate these oases of tranquility and beauty.

MELBA LEVICK

"Plant people are cool," remarked one garden manager in an offhand way. But the truth of that casual statement was confirmed time after time. Without exception, the people I met in the course of this project were cheerful, generous, and forthcoming.

Melba and I would like to thank those who introduced their gardens to us. At the estate gardens, John R. Copeland (Virginia Robinson Gardens); Dr. James Folsom (The Huntington Library, Art Collections, and Botanical Gardens); Pamela Seager (Rancho Los Alamitos); and Dr. Steven Timbrook (Lotusland). At the horticultural centers, George Lewis and Lynn Witherspoon (Descanso Gardens); Andy Morales and Ernest Mathis (Orcutt Ranch Horticulture Center); Wade Roberts (Sherman Library and Gardens); Kathy Puplava (Balboa Park); and Chuck Coburn (San Diego Zoo).

At the special purpose gardens, Steve Cutting and Denise Yarfitz (The J. Paul Getty Museum); Orlando Alayu and Jose Vara (Exposition Park Rose Garden); and Bruce Mars and Jack Hudkins (Self-Realization Fellowship Lake Shrine). At the Japanese gardens, Barry Prigge and Gabriel Aguilera (The UCLA Hannah Carter Japanese Garden); Virgil Hettick (Earl Burns Miller Japanese Garden); and Steve Harrington and Gene Greene (Donald C. Tillman Water Reclamation Plant Japanese Garden). At the desert gardens, Patricia Moorten (Moorten Botanical Garden) and Ruth Watling (The Living Desert).

At the botanic gardens, LuAnn Munz and John Provine (Los Angeles State and County Arboretum); Charles O'Neill (UC Irvine Arboretum); Dr. David L. Walkington, Rico Montenegro, and Dr. Frances Shropshire (Fullerton Arboretum); Dr. Mildred E. Mathias, Dave Verity, and John Hall (The Mildred E. Mathias Botanical Garden, UCLA); and Gilbert A. Voss (Quail Botanical Gardens). At the native gardens, Linda Aberbom, Dr. Steven Cohan, and Amy King (Rancho Santa Ana Botanic Garden); and Dr. David Young, Carol Bornstein, Dara Emery, Steve Junak, Janice Hartoch, and Abd al-Hayy Moore (Santa Barbara Botanic Garden).

I would like to thank the following librarians: Joan de Fato (Los Angeles State and County Arboretum), Barbara M. Pitschel (Strybing Arboretum), Michael Cart (Beverly Hills Public Library), Doris Mooney (Santa Barbara Public Library), Charles Shain (UC Berkeley College of Environmental Design), as well as the staffs of the Berkeley Public Library and the Oakland Public Library.

Thanks also to those who offered their enthusiasm and suggestions: Thomas A. Brown, Brad Bunnin, Robert Fletcher, Carol Greentree, Paul Groth, Petria MacDonnell, Drew Oman, Tom Sitton, Marvin Smith, Pat Stockard, and Liz Yamada. My special thanks to editor W. George Waters of *Pacific Horticulture*, stonemason Oswald Da Ros, landscape architect Ron Herman, and to publicist Dayna Macy who made the vital connection.

My personal appreciation to publisher Nion McEvoy, editor William LeBlond, who knew this book was for me, Carey Charlesworth for perceptive copy editing, Suzanne Kotz and Scott Hudson of Marquand Books for inspired book design, and Publicity Director Mary Ann Gilderbloom.

This book would not have been possible without the support of my family. Kay and Waller J. Prentice lovingly cared for my sons Asa and Graham when I needed time to travel, write, or recover. My parents Marjorie and George H. Kaplan offered wise counsel and encouragement. My husband Blair, colleague in design and my navigator in so many ways, made writing about Southern California a wonderful shared journey. We saw the gardens together.

HELAINE KAPLAN PRENTICE

A Note on the Sources

This book has drawn on many kinds of source material. Personal interviews were of the essence. These involved garden administrators, gardening crews, designers, builders, acquaintances of former owners, and ordinary visitors, as appropriate at each locale. Most facilities distribute interpretive literature free of charge upon arrival. These brochures, and the more substantial curatorial guides, provided a factual foundation. Newsletters offered a glimpse of garden membership, and when available, historic photographs and master plans permitted visualization of the gardens over time. Some garden makers have written books about their experiences, and these established context for the garden profiles.

The book of foremost importance to my inquiry into the topic as a whole was the classic account by Victoria Padilla, *Southern California Gardens*. Berkeley: University of California Press, 1961.

Other essential sources, as well as publications referenced in the profiles, are as follows:

Bartel, Janice R., and Sage Culpepper Belt. *A Guide to Botanical Resources of Southern California.* Los Angeles: Museum of Natural History, 1977.

Caldwell, Helen. *Ancient Poets Guide to UCLA Gardens.* Los Angeles: UCLA Botanical Gardens, 1968.

Dobyns, Winifred. *California Gardens.* New York: The Macmillan Company, 1931.

Getty, J. Paul. *As I See It.* Englewood Cliffs, NJ: Prentice-Hall, Inc., 1976.

Hodel, Donald R. *Exceptional Trees of Los Angeles.* Arcadia, CA: California Arboretum Foundation, Inc., 1988.

The Huntington Botanical Gardens 1905 … 1949: Personal Recollections of William Hertrich. San Marino, CA: Henry E. Huntington Library and Art Gallery, 1988.

The J. Paul Getty Museum Guide to the Villa and Its Gardens. Malibu: The J. Paul Getty Museum, 1988.

Jackson, Beverly. "Behind Lotusland Walls." *Santa Barbara News Press.* July 30, 1978.

Jekyll, Gertrude. *Colour Schemes for the Flower Garden.* Salem, NH: Ayre Co., 1983.

Lavender, David. "Historical Narrative." *Rancho Los Alamitos Interpretive Plan.* Long Beach: Rancho Los Alamitos Foundation, 1987.

Lenz, Lee W., and John Dourley. *California Native Trees and Shrubs.* Claremont: Rancho Santa Ana Botanic Garden, 1981.

Lockwood, Charles, and Peter V. Persic. *Greystone Historical Report.* Submitted to the Beverly Hills City Council, August 30, 1984.

McMahon, Marilyn. "Madame Lotusland." *Santa Barbara News Press.* January 26, 1986.

Montes, Gregory. "Balboa Park, 1909–1911: The Rise and Fall of the Olmsted Plan." *The Journal of San Diego History, 28,* no. 1, Winter 1982.

Moorten, Patricia, and Rex Nevins. *Desert Plants for Desert Gardens.* Palm Springs: Moorten Botanical Garden, 1973.

Munz, Philip A. *A Short History of the Rancho Santa Ana Botanic Garden.* Anaheim: Rancho Santa Ana Botanic Garden, 1947.

Munz, Philip A., and David D. Keck. *A California Flora and Supplement.* Berkeley and Los Angeles: University of California Press, 1968.

Nabhan, Gary. *Enduring Seeds.* San Francisco: North Point Press, 1989.

Pacific Horticulture: Journal of the Pacific Horticultural Foundation. Vols. 37–50, 1976–1989. W. George Waters, editor.

Schad, Robert O. *Henry Edwards Huntington: The Founder and the Library.* Reprinted from *The Huntington Library Bulletin, 1,* no. 1, May 1931.

Sitton, Tom. "Six Decades of 'Coming Up Roses': The Exposition Park Rose Garden." *TERRA, 26,* no. 1, Sept./Oct. 1987.

Smith, Thomas Gordon. *Classical Architecture: Rule and Invention.* Layton, UT: Gibbs M. Smith, 1988.

Streatfield, David C. "Historical Overview," *Rancho Los Alamitos Garden Restoration and Landscape Maintenance Plan.* Long Beach: Rancho Los Alamitos Foundation, 1987.

Treib, Marc, and Ron Herman. *A Guide to the Gardens of Kyoto.* Tokyo: Shufunotomo Co., Ltd., 1980.

The University Garden. Los Angeles: UCLA Botanical Gardens, 1969.

Wurman, Richard Saul. *LA/Access.* Los Angeles: Access Press, Inc., 1980.

Waters, W. George. "Lotusland." *Pacific Horticulture, 44,* no. 1, Spring 1983.

Walska, Ganna. *Always Room at the Top.* New York: Richard R. Smith, 1943.

Yogananda, Paramahansa. *Autobiography of a Yogi.* Los Angeles: Self-Realization Fellowship, 1972.

INDEX